T0201165

Fundamentals of Reliability Engineering

Scrivener Publishing
100 Cummings Center, Suite 541J
Beverly, MA 01915-6106

Performability Engineering Series
Series Editors: Krishna B. Misra (kbmisra@gmail.com)
and John Andrews (John.Andrews@nottingham.ac.uk)

Scope: A true performance of a product, or system, or service must be judged over the entire life cycle activities connected with design, manufacture, use and disposal in relation to the economics of maximization of dependability, and minimizing its impact on the environment. The concept of performability allows us to take a holistic assessment of performance and provides an aggregate attribute that reflects an entire engineering effort of a product, system, or service designer in achieving dependability and sustainability. Performance should not just be indicative of achieving quality, reliability, maintainability and safety for a product, system, or service, but achieving sustainability as well. The conventional perspective of dependability ignores the environmental impact considerations that accompany the development of products, systems, and services. However, any industrial activity in creating a product, system, or service is always associated with certain environmental impacts that follow at each phase of development. These considerations have become all the more necessary in the 21st century as the world resources continue to become scarce and the cost of materials and energy keep rising. It is not difficult to visualize that by employing the strategy of dematerialization, minimum energy and minimum waste, while maximizing the yield and developing economically viable and safe processes (clean production and clean technologies), we will create minimal adverse effect on the environment during production and disposal at the end of the life. This is basically the goal of performability engineering.

It may be observed that the above-mentioned performance attributes are interrelated and should not be considered in isolation for optimization of performance. Each book in the series should endeavor to include most, if not all, of the attributes of this web of interrelationship and have the objective to help create optimal and sustainable products, systems, and services.

Publishers at Scrivener
Martin Scrivener (martin@scrivenerpublishing.com)
Phillip Carmical (pcarmical@scrivenerpublishing.com)

Fundamentals of Reliability Engineering

Applications in Multistage Interconnection Networks

Indra Gunawan

Federation University Australia

Scrivener
Publishing

WILEY

Co-published by John Wiley & Sons, Inc. Hoboken, New Jersey, and Scrivener Publishing LLC, Salem, Massachusetts.
Published simultaneously in Canada.

For general information on our other products and services or for technical support, please contact our Customer Care Department within the United States at (800) 762-2974, outside the United States at (317) 572-3993 or fax (317) 572-4002.

Wiley also publishes its books in a variety of electronic formats. Some content that appears in print may not be available in electronic formats. For more information about Wiley products, visit our web site at www.wiley.com.

For more information about Scrivener products please visit www.scrivenerpublishing.com.

Cover design by Exeter Premedia Services Private Ltd., Chennai, India

Library of Congress Cataloging-in-Publication Data:

ISBN 978-1-118-54956-8

Printed in the United States of America

10 9 8 7 6 5 4 3 2 1

Contents

Preface

The purpose of this book is to provide readers with fundamentals of reliability engineering and demonstrate reliability approaches for evaluating system reliability with case studies in multistage interconnection networks.

The book can be used as an introductory book in reliability engineering for undergraduate/graduate students in Industrial/Electrical/Computer Engineering as well as engineers, researchers or managers. Practical applications are included to describe the importance of reliability measurement to achieve better systems.

In the first part of the book (chapters 1-5), it introduces the concept of reliability engineering, elements of probability theory, probability distributions, availability and data analysis.

The second part of the book (chapters 6-11) provides an overview of parallel/distributed computing, network design considerations, classification of multistage interconnection networks, network reliability evaluation methods, and reliability analysis of multistage interconnection networks including reliability prediction of distributed systems using Monte Carlo method.

It covers comprehensive reliability engineering methods and practical aspects in interconnection network systems. Students, engineers, researchers, managers will find this book as a valuable reference source.

The main key features of this book include:

- Fundamental of reliability engineering.
- Elements of probability and probability distributions.
- Classification of network systems.
- Reliability evaluation methods.
- Reliability analysis of multistage interconnection network systems is illustrated as practical applications of reliability methods including reliability prediction of distributed systems using Monte Carlo method.

I would like to express my gratitude to Prof. K.B. Misra for his kind assistance in reviewing the book.

Finally, my heartfelt thanks go to my wife Donna, daughters Jessica and Cynthia for their continuous support and my parents Suwita and Effie Gunawan for their motivation and encouragement.

1

Introduction to Reliability Engineering

Reliability is defined as the probability that a system (part or component) can perform its intended task under specified conditions and time interval. It is used normally as the quantitative measure of the performance of a designed part, component or system. Reliability is also a design parameter which can be improved by design modification, redesign, elimination of deficiencies, and addition of redundant components or units.

The first part of this book (chapters 1–5) describes fundamentals of reliability engineering and the second part (chapters 6–11) presents reliability methods and its applications in Multistage Interconnection Networks (MIN). Chapter 9–11 discusses in details reliability analysis of network systems. Reliability of MIN is an important parameter that can be used as a measure on how reliable the interconnected components in network systems.

1.1　The Logic of Certainty

Event is a statement that can be true or false. "It may rain today" is not an event. According to our current state of knowledge, we may say that an event is true, false, or possible (uncertain). Eventually, an event will be either true or false.

Sample Space is the set of all possible outcomes of an experiment [1–4]. Each elementary outcome is represented by a sample point. Examples: there are six possible outcomes/numbers {1, 2, 3, 4, 5, 6} from tossing a die; the failure time of a component is {0,∞}. A collection of sample points is an event.

Indicator variables for events can be written in the following form. If an event i is true then $X_i = 1$ and if an event i is false then $X_i = 0$. Two basic operations, Union (OR) and Intersection (AND) are discussed.

1.2   Union (OR) operation

Suppose there are two events, A and B in the sample space. The equations below represent C as a union of the two events. $X_C = 1$ means that an event C is true when either event A or B is true.

$$A \cup B = C \tag{1.1}$$

$$X_C = 1 - (1 - X_A)(1 - X_B) \tag{1.2}$$

$$X_C \equiv \coprod X_j \tag{1.3}$$

Diagram Venn and fault tree for union (OR) operations are shown in Figure 1.1 below.

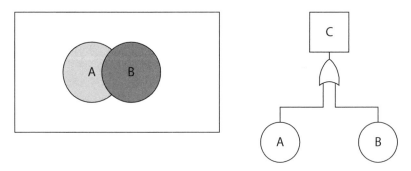

Figure 1.1 Diagram Venn and Fault Tree for Union (OR) Operation.

1.3   Intersection (AND) operation

The equations below represent C as an intersection of A and B. $X_C = 1$ means that an event C is true when both the events are true.

$$A \cap B = C \tag{1.4}$$

$$X_C = X_A X_B \tag{1.5}$$

$$X_C \equiv \prod X_j \tag{1.6}$$

Diagram Venn and fault tree for intersection (AND) operations are shown in Figure 1.2 below.

In A and B are mutually exclusive events (they are independent to each other) then

$$A \cap B = \varnothing \tag{1.7}$$

These two basic operations are implemented in real systems as below.

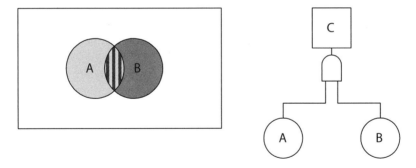

Figure 1.2 Diagram Venn and Fault Tree for Intersection (AND) Operation.

1.4   Series systems

Structure function of system failure and success in series systems can be defined as follows:
System failure:

$$X = 1 - \prod_{1}^{N} (1 - X_j) \equiv \prod_{1}^{N} X_j \qquad (1.8)$$

System success:

$$Y = \prod_{1}^{N} Y_j \qquad (1.9)$$

Where $X_j = 1$ or $Y_j = 1$ represent when the component j is failed or working.

Reliability block diagram and fault tree for series systems are shown in Figure 1.3 below.

The system reliability Rs is the product of the individual element reliabilities:

$$Rs = R_1 \times R_2 \times R_3 \times \dots R_N \qquad (1.10)$$

If we assume that each of the elements has a constant failure rate, then the reliability of the i_{th} element is given by the exponential relation:

$$R_i = e^{-\lambda_i t} \qquad (1.11)$$

Thus,

$$R_s = e^{-\lambda_1 t} e^{-\lambda_2 t} \dots e^{-\lambda_i t} \dots e^{-\lambda_N t}$$
$$R_s = e^{-\lambda_s t} = e^{-(\lambda_1 + \lambda_2 + \dots + \lambda_i + \dots + \lambda_N)t} \qquad (1.12)$$

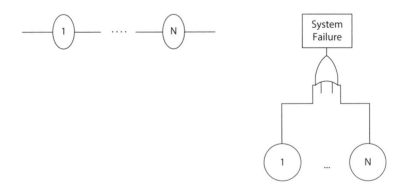

Figure 1.3 Reliability Block Diagram and Fault Tree for Series Systems.

and failure rate of system of N elements in series

$$\lambda_s = \lambda_1 + \lambda_2 + ... + \lambda_i + ... + \lambda_N \tag{1.13}$$

Since $R_s = 1 - F_s$ and $R_i = 1 - F_i$
Then
$1 - F_s = (1 - F_1)(1 - F_2) ... (1 - F_i) ... (1 - F_N)$
$\quad = 1 - (F_1 + F_2 + ... F_{1+} + F_N) + \text{products of the F's}$
If the individual F_i are small, i.e. $F_i \ll 1$,

$$F_s \approx F_1 + F_2 + ... + F_i + ... + F_N \tag{1.14}$$

1.5   Parallel systems

Structure function of system failure and success in parallel systems can be defined as follows:
System failure:

$$X = \prod_1^N X_j \tag{1.15}$$

System success:

$$Y = \coprod_1^N Y_j \tag{1.16}$$

Where $X_j = 1$ or $Y_j = 1$ represent when the component j is failed or working.
    Reliability block diagram and fault tree for parallel systems are shown in Figure 1.4 below.

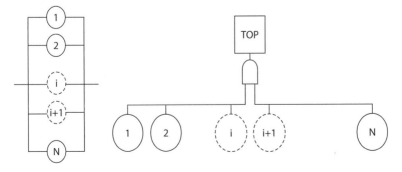

Figure 1.4 Reliability Block Diagram and Fault Tree for Parallel Systems.

The unreliability of parallel system is given by:

$$F_s = F_1 F_2 ... F_i ... F_N \qquad (1.17)$$

If the individual elements are identical:

$$F_1 = F_2 = ... = F_i = ... = F_N = F \qquad (1.18)$$

This gives:

$$F_s = F^n$$

1.6   General Series-Parallel System

A general series-parallel system consists of n identical subsystems in parallel and each subsystem consists of m elements in series.

If R_{ji} is the reliability of the ith elements in the jth subsystem, then the reliability of the jth subsystem is:

$$R_j = R_{j1} R_{j2} ... R_{ji} ... R_{jm} = \prod_{i=1}^{i=m} R_{ji} \qquad (1.19)$$

The corresponding unreliability of the jth subsystem is:

$$F_j = 1 - \prod_{i=1}^{i=m} R_{ji} \qquad (1.20)$$

The overall system unreliability is:

$$F_o = \prod_{j=1}^{j=n} \left[1 - \prod_{i=1}^{i=m} R_{ji} \right] \qquad (1.21)$$

1.7   Active Redundancy

A system is referred to as "k out of n" if the overall system will continue to function correctly when only k ($k \leq n$) of the n elements/systems are working normally; the remaining (n – k) elements/systems ensure extra reliability.

In 2 out of 4 system, the overall system unreliability is:

F = Prob. (A,B,C,D fail) + Prob. (A,B,C fail) + Prob. (B,C,D fail) + Prob. (A,C,D fail) + Prob. (A,B,D fail)

$$F = F^4 + F^3R + F^3R + F^3R + F^3R$$

$$= F^4 + 4F^3R$$

$$= F^3 (F + 4R) \tag{1.22}$$

The above result can also be obtained from the binomial expansion of $(F + R)^4$:

$$(F + R)^4 = F^4 + 4F^3R + 6F^2R^2 + 4FR^3 + R^4 \tag{1.23}$$

If R is very close to 1 and F a lot smaller than 1, then:

$$F = 4F^3 \tag{1.24}$$

1.8   Standby Redundancy

In this system, only one unit is operating at a time; the other units are shut down and are only brought into operation when the operating unit fails.

Assuming the switching system has perfect reliability, then the reliability of the standby system can be given by the cumulative Poisson distribution [5]:

$$R(t) = \exp(-\lambda t) \sum_{k=0}^{n-1} \frac{(\lambda t)^k}{k!} \tag{1.25}$$

Thus for $n = 1$, $R(t) = \exp(-\lambda t)$
For n = 2, $R(t)$ is increased to:
$R(t) = \exp(-\lambda t) [1 + \lambda t]$
The term $\exp(-\lambda t) [\lambda t]$ represents the increase in reliability due to adding one standby unit.
For n = 3, $R(t)$ is further increase to:

$$R(t) = \exp(-\lambda t)[1 + \lambda t + \frac{1}{2}(\lambda t)^2]$$

1.9   Fault Tree Analysis

A k out of n system means that at least k components should be working for the system to be operational. An example 2 out of 3 system is described in Figure 1.5 below:

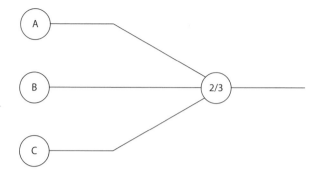

Figure 1.5 Reliability Block Diagram for 2 out of 3 system.

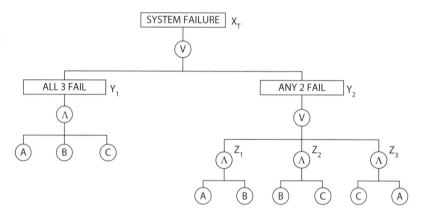

Figure 1.6 Fault Tree Diagram for 2 out of 3 system.

Fault tree diagram is used to represent how the structure of the system works [6–7]. Fault tree diagram for this system is shown in Figure 1.6 above (symbol V represents OR operation and ∧ represents AND operation):

Structure function for system failure can be formulated as follows:

$$X_T = 1 - (1 - Y_1)(1 - Y_2)$$
$$= 1 - (1 - X_A X_B X_C)\{1 - [1 - (1 - Z_1)(1 - Z_2)(1 - Z_3)]\}$$
$$= 1 - (1 - X_A X_B X_C)\{1 - [1 - (1 - X_A X_B)(1 - X_B X_C)(1 - X_C X_A)]\}$$

Expanding and using $X^k = X$ we get

$$X_T = 1 - (1 - X_A X_B)(1 - X_B X_C)(1 - X_C X_A)$$ (1.26)

1.10   Minimum Cut Sets and Path Sets

Cut Set is any set of events (failures of components and human actions) that cause system failure [8–9]. Minimal cut set is a cut set that does not contain another cut set as a subset. On the other hand, Path Set represents any set of events that cause system success.

For 2 out of 3 system, we now can simplify the fault tree diagram into Figure 1.7 below: $M_1 = X_A X_B$, $\quad M_2 = X_B X_C$,, $\quad M_3 = X_C X_A$ Minimal cut sets:

$$X_T = \coprod_1^3 M_j \equiv 1 - (1 - M_1)(1 - M_2)(1 - M_3) =$$
$$= 1 - (1 - X_A X_B)(1 - X_B X_C)(1 - X_C X_A)$$

Another method to find the system failure function is by using the following formula:

$$X_T = \sum_{i=1}^{N} M_i - \sum_{i=1}^{N-1} \sum_{j=i+1}^{N} M_i M_j + \ldots + (-1)^{N+1} \prod_{i=1}^{N} M_i$$ (1.27)

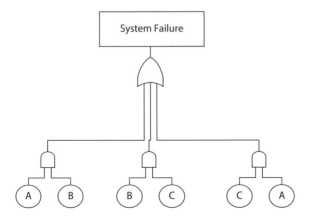

Figure 1.7 Simplified Fault Tree Diagram for 2 out of 3 system.

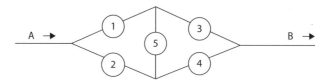

Figure1.8 Bridge System

$$X_T = 1-(1-X_A X_B)\,(1-X_B X_C)\,(1-X_C X_A)$$
$$X_T = (M_1 + M_2 + M_3) - (M_1 M_2 + M_2 M_3 + M_3 M_1) + M_1 M_2 M_3$$
Where:
$$M_1 M_2 = X_A X_B{}^2 X_C = X_A X_B X_C$$
Therefore:
$$X_T = (X_A X_B + X_B X_C + X_C X_A) - 2X_A X_B X_C$$

This minimum cut set approach can be applied to find the system failure of the bridge system as shown in Figure 1.8 above:

There are four minimum cut sets for this system: $\{X_1 X_2\}$, $\{X_3 X_4\}$, $\{X_2 X_3 X_5\}$, $\{X_1 X_4 X_5\}$

Therefore the system failure function can be written as:

$$X_T = 1-(1-X_1 X_2)(1-X_3 X_4)(1-X_2 X_3 X_5)(1-X_1 X_4 X_5) =$$
$$X_1 X_2 + X_3 X_4 + X_2 X_3 X_5 + X_1 X_4 X_5 - X_1 X_2 X_3 X_4 - X_1 X_2 X_3 X_5$$
$$- X_1 X_2 X_4 X_5 - X_2 X_3 X_4 X_5 - X_1 X_3 X_4 X_5 + 2X_1 X_2 X_3 X_4 X_5 \qquad (1.28)$$

References

1. Walpole, R.E., Myers, R.H., and Myers, S.L., *Probability and Statistics for Engineers and Scientists*, Sixth edition, Prentice Hall, 1998.
2. Montgomery, D.C. and Runger, G.C., *Applied Statistics and Probability for Engineers*, Second edition, John Wiley & Sons, Inc., 1999.
3. Ross, S.M., *Introduction to Probability Models*, Sixth edition, Academic Press, 1999.
4. Montgomery, D.C., Runger, G.C., and Hubele, N.F., *Engineering Statistics*, John Wiley & Sons, Inc., 1998.
5. Bentley, J., *Introduction to Reliability and Quality Engineering*, Second edition, Pearson, 1999.
6. Rausand, M. and Hoyland, A., *System Reliability Theory: Models, Statistical Methods, and Applications*, John Wiley & Sons, Inc., 2004.
7. Kumamoto, H. and Henley, E.J., *Probabilistic Risk Assessment and Management for Engineers and Scientists*, Second edition, IEEE Press, 1996.
8. Misra, K.B., *Reliability Prediction and Analysis: A Methodology Oriented Treatment*, Elsevier, 1992.
9. Misra, K.B., *New Trends in System Reliability Evaluation*, Elsevier, 1993.

2

Elements of Probability Theory

2.1 Basic Rules of Probability

The probability of an event A is a quantity that satisfies the following axioms [1–5]:

$0 \leq P(A) \leq 1$ where $P(\text{certain event}) = 1$

For two events $P(A \cup B) = P(A) + P(B) - P(AB)$ and for two mutually exclusive events A and B $P(A \text{ or } B) = P(A) + P(B)$

In general,

$$P\left(\bigcup_1^N A_i\right) = \sum_{i=1}^N P(A_i) - \sum_{i=1}^{N-1}\sum_{j=i+1}^N P(A_i A_j) +$$

$$\ldots + (-1)^{N+1} P\left(\bigcap_1^N A_i\right) \qquad (2.1)$$

For the rare event approximation,

$$P\left(\bigcup_1^N A_i\right) \cong \sum_{i=1}^N P(A_i) \qquad (2.2)$$

Example: when a die is tossed, the outcomes are equally likely (1/6). P(even) = P(2 ∪ 4 ∪ 6) = ½ (mutually exclusive).

2.2   Cumulative Distribution Function

The cumulative distribution function (CDF) is $F(x) \equiv \Pr[X \leq x]$. This is valid for both discrete and continuous random variables.
Properties:

1. F(x) is a non-decreasing function of x.
2. $F(-\infty) = 0$
3. $F(\infty) = 1$

2.3   Probability Mass Function

For discrete random variable (DRV), probability mass function is $P(X = x_i) \equiv p_i$.

$$F(x) = \sum p_i, \quad \text{for all and} \sum_i p_i = 1 \tag{2.3}$$

2.4   Probability Density Function

For continuous random variable (CRV), probability density function (PDF) is defined as:

$$f(x) = \frac{dF(x)}{dx} \tag{2.4}$$

$$F(x) = \int_{-\infty}^{x} f(s)ds \tag{2.5}$$

$$F(\infty) = \int_{-\infty}^{\infty} f(s)ds = 1 \tag{2.6}$$

Example: Determine k so that $f(x) = kx^2, \quad for \ 0 \leq x \leq 1$
$f(x) = 0$, otherwise.

The normalization condition gives $\int_{0}^{1} kx^2 dx = 1 \implies k = 3$

$$F(x) = x^3$$

$$F(0.875) - F(0.75) = \int_{0.75}^{0.875} 3x^2 dx = 0.67 - 0.42 = 0.25 = P\{0.75 < X < 0.875\}$$

2.5   Moments

Expected (or mean, or average) value:

$$E[x] \equiv m \equiv \begin{cases} \int_{-\infty}^{\infty} x f(x) dx & CRV \qquad (2.7) \\ \sum_j x_j p_j & DRV \qquad (2.8) \end{cases}$$

Variance (standard deviation σ):

$$E\left[(x-m)^2\right] \equiv \sigma^2 = \begin{cases} \int_{-\infty}^{\infty} (x-m)^2 f(x) dx & CRV \qquad (2.9) \\ \sum_j (x_j - m)^2 p_j & DRV \qquad (2.10) \end{cases}$$

2.6   Percentiles

Median: The value x_m for which $F(x_m) = 0.50$
For continuous random variable, the 100γ percentile is defined as that value of x for which

$$\int_{-\infty}^{x_\gamma} f(x) dx = \gamma \qquad (2.11)$$

Example:

$$m = \int_0^1 3x^3 dx = 0.75$$

$$\sigma^2 = \int_0^1 3(x - 0.75)^2 x^2 dx = 0.0375$$

$$\sigma = 0.194$$

$$x_{0.05}^3 = 0.05 \qquad \Rightarrow \qquad x_{0.05} = 0.37$$

$$x_{0.95}^3 = 0.95 \qquad \Rightarrow \qquad x_{0.95} = 0.98$$

References

1. O'Connor, P.D.T. and Kleyner, A., *Practical Reliability Engineering*, Fifth Edition, John Wiley & Sons, Ltd., 2012.
2. Walpole, R.E., Myers, R.H., and Myers, S.L., *Probability and Statistics for Engineers and Scientists*, Sixth edition, Prentice Hall, 1998.
3. Montgomery, D.C. and Runger, G.C., *Applied Statistics and Probability for Engineers*, Second edition, John Wiley & Sons, Inc., 1999.
4. Ross, S.M., *Introduction to Probability Models*, Sixth edition, Academic Press, 1999.
5. Montgomery, D.C., Runger, G.C., and Hubele, N.F., *Engineering Statistics*, John Wiley & Sons, Inc., 1998.

3

Probability Distributions

In this chapter, characteristics of discrete probability distributions such as binomial and poisson as well as common continuous probability distributions such as exponential, weibull, normal and lognormal are discussed [1-6].

These distributions are needed to formulate:

- The probability that a component will start (fail) on demand.
- The probability that a component will run for a period of time given a successful start.
- The impact of repair on these probabilities.
- The frequency of initiating events.

In general, it can be defined that:

- P[failure to start on demand] $\equiv q \equiv$ unavailability
- P[successful start on demand] $\equiv p \equiv$ availability
- Requirement: $p + q = 1$

3.1   Binomial

- Binomial probability distribution can be applied to an "experiment" that can have only two outcomes: "success" and "failure" or {0, 1} with probabilities p and q, respectively.
- Consider N "trials," i.e., repetitions of this experiment with constant q. These are called *Bernoulli trials*.
- Define a new Discrete Random Variable (DRV): X = number of 1's in N trials
- Sample space of X: {0,1,2,...,N}
- The probability that there will be k 1's (failures) in N trials is

$$\Pr[X = k] = \binom{N}{k} q^k (1-q)^{N-k} \qquad (3.1)$$

- This is the probability mass function (PMF) of the Binomial Distribution.
- It is the probability of *exactly* k failures in N demands.
- The *binomial coefficient* is:

$$\binom{N}{k} \equiv \frac{N!}{k!(N-k)!} \qquad (3.2)$$

- Mean number of failures:

$$qN \qquad (3.3)$$

- Variance:

$$q(1-q)N \qquad (3.4)$$

Normalization:

$$\sum_{k=0}^{N} \binom{N}{k} q^k (1-q)^{N-k} = 1 \qquad (3.5)$$

P[at most m failures] =

$$\sum_{k=0}^{m} \binom{N}{k} q^k (1-q)^{N-k} \qquad (3.6)$$

Example: 2-out-of-3 system

- We found that the structure function is (using min cut sets):
  $X_T = (X_A X_B + X_B X_C + X_C X_A) - 2X_A X_B X_C$
- The failure probability is P(failure) = $P(X_T=1) = 3q^2 - 2q^3$
- Using the binomial distribution:
  Pr(system failure) = P[2 fail] + P[3 fail] = $3q^2(1-q) + q^3$
  $= 3q^2 - 2q^3$

3.2   Poisson

- Used typically to model the occurrence of initiating events.
- DRV: number of events in (0, t)
- Rate is constant; the events are independent.
- The probability of exactly k events in (0, t) is (PMF):

$$Pr[k] = e^{-\lambda t} \frac{(\lambda t)^k}{k!} \tag{3.7}$$

$k! \equiv 1*2*\ldots*(k-1)*k \ \ 0! = 1$

$$m = \lambda t \tag{3.8}$$

$$\sigma^2 = \lambda t \tag{3.9}$$

Example of the Poisson Distribution

- A component fails due to "shocks" that occur, on the average, once every 100 hours. What is the probability of exactly one replacement in 100 hours? Of no replacement?
- $\lambda t = 10^{-2}*100 = 1$
- Pr[1 repl.] = e-λt = e-1 = 0.37 = Pr[no replacement]
- Expected number of replacements: 1

$$Pr[2repl] = e^{-1} \frac{1^2}{2!} = \frac{e^{-1}}{2} = 0.185$$

Pr[k≤2] = 0.37 + 0.37 + 0.185 = 0.925
Failure while running

- T: the time to failure of a component.
- F(t) = P[T < t]: failure distribution (unreliability)
- R(t) $\equiv$ 1-F(t) = P[t < T]: reliability

- m: mean time to failure (MTTF)
- f(t): failure density, f(t)dt = P{failure occurs between t and t+dt} = P [t < T < t+dt]

3.3   Exponential

- $f(t) = \lambda e^{-\lambda t}$ 0, t > 0 (failure density) (3.10)

- $F(t) = 1 - e^{-\lambda t}$ (3.11)

- $R(t) = e^{-\lambda t}$ (3.12)

- h(t) = constant (no memory; the *only* pdf with this property) with useful life on bathtub curve

F(t) ≅ λt for t < 0.1 (*another* rare-event approximation) (3.13)

$$m = \frac{1}{\lambda} = \sigma \qquad (3.14)$$

Example: 2-out-of-3 system
Each sensor has a MTTF equal to 2,000 hours. What is the unreliability of the system for a period of 720 hours?

- Step 1: System Logic.

$X_T = (X_A X_B + X_B X_C + X_C X_A) - 2X_A X_B X_C$

- Step 2: Probabilistic Analysis.

For nominally identical components:
P(XT) = 3q2 − 2q3
But $q(t) = 1 - e^{-\lambda t} = F(t)$ with $\lambda = 5 \times 10^{-4}$ hr^{-1}
System Unreliability: $F_T(t) = 3(1 - e^{-\lambda t})2 - 2(1 - e^{-\lambda t})^3$
If λt < 0.1 ⇒ $F_T \cong 3(\lambda t)^2 - 2(\lambda t)^3$
For λ = 5x10⁻⁴ hr⁻¹ and t = 720 hrs ⇒ λt = 0.36 ⇒
$q(t) = 1 - e^{-\lambda t} = 0.30 \Rightarrow F_T(720) = 3 \times 0.30^2 - 2 \times 0.30^3 = 0.22$
Since λt = 0.36 > 0.1 ⇒ the rare-event approximation does not apply.
Indeed, $F_T \cong 3(\lambda t)^2 - 2(\lambda t)^3 \Rightarrow F_T(720) \cong 3 \times 0.36^2 - 2 \times 0.36^3 = 0.295 > 0.2$

3.4   Weibull

The Weibull instantaneous failure rate or hazard function is given by:

$$\lambda(t) = \frac{\beta}{\eta}\left(\frac{t-t_0}{\eta}\right)^{\beta-1}, \beta > 0 \tag{3.15}$$

where:

t_0 determines the position of the origin
$(R(t_0) = 1$ at $t = t_0$
η is the scale parameter
β is the shape parameter

$$R(t) = \exp\left\{-\left(\frac{t-t_0}{\eta}\right)^{\beta}\right\} \tag{3.16}$$

If we assume $\tau = (t - t_0)/\eta$,
where τ is normalized time, then:

$$\eta\lambda(\tau) = \beta\tau^{\beta-1}$$
$$R(\tau) = \exp(-\tau^{\beta})$$

3.5   Normal

Probability density function (PDF) of normal distribution can be defined as below:

$$f(x) = \frac{1}{\sqrt{2\pi}\sigma}\exp[-\frac{(x-\mu)^2}{2\sigma^2}] \tag{3.17}$$

Where:

$-\infty < x < \infty,$

$-\infty < \mu < \infty,$

$0 < \sigma < \infty$

Mean: μ Standard Deviation: σ
Standard Normal Variable:

$$Z = \frac{X-\mu}{\sigma} \tag{3.18}$$

Standard Normal Distribution:

$$\phi(z) = \frac{1}{\sqrt{2\pi}} \exp[-\frac{z^2}{2}] \tag{3.19}$$

Example of the normal distribution:

- $\mu = 10{,}000$ hr (MTTF) = 1,000 hr
- Pr $[X > 11{,}000$ hr] = Pr $[Z > 1] = 0.50 - 0.34 = 0.16$

$$Z = \frac{11{,}000 - 10{,}000}{1{,}000} = 1$$

An Example

A capacitor is placed across a power source. Assume that surge voltages occur on the line at a rate of one per month and they are normally distributed with a mean value of 100 volts and a standard deviation of 15 volts. The breakdown voltage of the capacitor is 130 volts.

i.   Find the mean time to failure (MTTF) for this capacitor.

λ_{SV} = 1 per month

$P_{d/sv}$ = conditional probability of damage given a surge voltage = P (surge voltage>130 volts/surge voltage) =

$$= P(Z > \frac{130 - 100}{15}) = P(Z > 2) =$$

$$= 1 - P(Z < 2) = 1 - 0.9772 = 0.0228$$

Therefore, the rate of damaging surge voltages is

$\lambda_d = \lambda_{SV} \times P_{d/sv} = 2.28 \times 10^{-2}$ per month

Equivalently, the capacitor's failure time follows an exponential distribution with rate

MTTF = 43.86 months

ii.   Find the capacitor's reliability for a time period of three months.

R(3 mos) = exp$(- \lambda_d \times 3)$ = exp$(-2.28 \times 10^{-2} \times 3)$ = 0.934

3.6   Lognormal

$$\pi(\lambda) = \frac{1}{\sqrt{2\pi}\sigma\lambda} \exp\left[-\frac{(\ln \lambda - \mu)^2}{2\sigma^2}\right] \tag{3.20}$$

$$mean : m = \exp\left[\mu + \frac{\sigma^2}{2}\right]$$

(3.21)

$$median : \lambda_{50} = e^{\mu}$$

(3.22)

$$\lambda_{95} = e^{\mu + 1.645\sigma}$$

(3.23)

$$\lambda_{05} = e^{\mu - 1.645\sigma}$$

(3.24)

Error Factor:

$$EF = \frac{\lambda_{95}}{\lambda_{50}} = \frac{\lambda_{50}}{\lambda_{05}} = \sqrt{\frac{\lambda_{95}}{\lambda_{05}}}$$

(3.25)

Relationship with the Normal Distribution
If λ is a lognormal variable with parameters μ and σ,
then:

$$Y \equiv \ln \lambda$$

is a normal variable with parameters μ (mean) and σ (standard deviation).
The 95th percentile
Since Y is a normal variable, its 95th percentile is
   $Y_{95} = \mu + 1.645 \mu$
But, $Y \equiv \ln l \Rightarrow \ln = \mu + 1.645 \mu \Rightarrow$

$$\lambda_{95} = e^{\mu + 1.645\sigma}$$

An example of the Lognormal Distribution:
Suppose that $\mu = -6.91$ and $\sigma = 1.40$

- Median: $\lambda_{50} = \exp(-6.91) \cong 10^{-3}$
- Mean: $m = \exp(-6.91 + 1.40^2/2) = 2.65 \times 10^{-3}$
- 95th percentile: $= \lambda_{95} \exp(-6.91 + 1.645 \times 1.40) \cong 10^{-2}$
- 5th percentile: $\lambda_{05} = \exp(-6.91 - 1.645 \times 1.40) \cong 10^{-4}$
- Error Factor: EF = 10

3.7 Mean Time To Failure (MTTF)

Reliability (R) is the probability that the product continues to meet the specification, over a given time period, subject to given environmental conditions.

Unreliability (F) is the probability that the product fails to meet the specification.

R(t) + F(t) = 1

MTTF for non-repairable and repairable items are presented [7].

Non-repairable items

Assume that all N items fail during a test interval T and the *ith* failure occurs at time T_i

T_i is the survival time or up time for the ith failure.
Mean time to failure (MTTF):

$$\text{MTTF} = \frac{\text{Total up time}}{\text{Number of failures}} = \frac{1}{N}\sum_{i=1}^{i=N}T_i \qquad (3.26)$$

The mean failure rate $\bar{\lambda}$:

$$\bar{\lambda} = \frac{\text{Number of failures}}{\text{Total up time}} = \frac{N}{\sum_{i=1}^{i=N}T_i} = \frac{1}{\text{MTTF}} \qquad (3.27)$$

For the continuous function R(t):

$$\text{MTTF} = \int_0^{\infty} R(t)\,dt \qquad (3.28)$$

Repairable items

The down time T_{Dj} associated with the j_{th} failure is the total time that elapses between the occurrence of the failure and the repaired item being put back into normal operation.

Mean down time (MDT):

$$\text{MDT} = \frac{\text{Total down time}}{\text{Number of failures}} = \frac{1}{N_F} \sum_{j=1}^{j=N_F} T_{Dj} \qquad (3.29)$$

$$\text{Total up time} = \text{NT} - \sum_{j=1}^{j=N_F} T_{Dj} = \text{NT} - N_F \text{MDT} \qquad (3.30)$$

The mean up time or the mean time between failures (MTBF) is therefore given by:

$$\text{MTBF} = \text{Total up time} / \text{Number of failures} =$$
$$NT - N_F MDT/N_F \qquad (3.31)$$

The mean failure rate is given by:

$$\text{Mean failure rate } \bar{\lambda} = \frac{\text{Number of failures}}{\text{Total up time}} = \frac{N_F}{NT - N_F \text{MDT}} \qquad (3.32)$$

References

1. Lewis, E. E., *Introduction to Reliability Engineering*, Second Edition, John Wiley & Sons, Ltd., 1994.
2. O'Connor, P.D.T. and Kleyner, A., *Practical Reliability Engineering*, Fifth Edition, John Wiley & Sons, Ltd., 2012.
3. Walpole, R.E., Myers, R.H., and Myers, S.L., *Probability and Statistics for Engineers and Scientists*, Sixth edition, Prentice Hall, 1998.
4. Montgomery, D.C. and Runger, G.C., *Applied Statistics and Probability for Engineers*, Second edition, John Wiley & Sons, Inc., 1999.
5. Ross, S.M., *Introduction to Probability Models*, Sixth edition, Academic Press, 1999.
6. Montgomery, D.C., Runger, G.C., and Hubele, N.F., *Engineering Statistics*, John Wiley & Sons, Inc., 1998.
7. Bentley, J., *Introduction to Reliability and Quality Engineering*, Second edition, Pearson, 1999.

4

Availability

4.1 Definition

Unavailability is defined as $q(t) = \Pr[\text{down at } t]$
Availability [1–4] can be calculated as $p(t) \equiv 1-q(t) = \Pr[\text{up at } t]$
$q(t) + p(t) = 1$

For unattended components:
$q(t) = F(t) = \Pr[T < t]$

Example: 2-out-of-3 system of exponential components
$Q_s(t) = F_s(t) = 3(1-e^{-\lambda t})^2 - 2(1-e^{-\lambda t})^3$

In general continuously monitored repairable components, the random sequence of uptimes and downtimes can be represented in Figure 4.1 below:

Average unavailability: $q = \dfrac{MTTR}{MTTF + MTTR}$

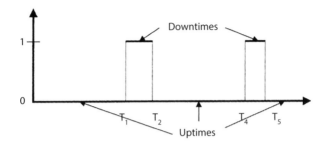

Figure 4.1 Continuously monitored repairable components.

For the exponential failure distribution:

$$MTTF = \frac{1}{\lambda}$$

$$q = \frac{\tau}{\tau + \dfrac{1}{\lambda}} = \frac{\lambda\tau}{1+\lambda\tau}, \quad Note: \quad q \cong \lambda\tau \quad for \quad \lambda\tau < 0.1$$

Example:

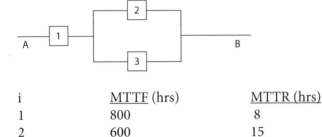

i	MTTF (hrs)	MTTR (hrs)
1	800	8
2	600	15
3	600	15

What is the reliability of the system for one month assuming that no repair is available?

Step 1: System Logic

Minimal path sets: $\{Y_1, Y_2\}$ $\{Y_1, Y_3\}$

Structure function for success:

$$Y_S = 1 - (1 - Y_1 Y_2)(1 - Y_1 Y_3)$$
$$Y_S = Y_1(Y_2 + Y_3 - Y_2 Y_3)$$

Step 2: Reliability of the system in terms of component reliabilities:

$$R_S = R_1(R_2 + R_3 - R_2 R_3)$$

Component reliabilities:
$R_1 = \exp(-720/800) = 0.407$
$R_2 = R_3 = \exp(-720/600) = 0.301$

Therefore, $R_S = 0.208$

What is the availability of the system assuming that the repair process starts immediately upon detection of failure?
Structure function for success
$Y_S = Y_1(Y_2 + Y_3 - Y_2 Y_3)$
Availability of the system in terms of component availabilities:
$P_S = P_1(P_2 + P_3 - P_2 P_3)$

Component availabilities:
$p_1 = 1 - (8/800) = 0.990$
$p_2 = p_3 = 1 - (15/600) = 0.975.$
Therefore, $P_S = 0.989.$

Minimal cut sets: X_1 and $X_2 X_3$
Structure function for failure:
$X_S = 1 - (1 - X_1)(1 - X_2 X_3)$
$X_S = X_1 + X_2 X_3 - X_1 X_2 X_3$

The unreliability of the system for one month is:
$F_S = F_1 + F_2 F_3 - F_1 F_2 F_3$
where: $F_1 = 1 - \exp(-720/800) = 0.593$
$F_2 = F_3 = 1 - \exp(-720/600) = 0.699.$
Thus,
$F_S = 0.792 = 1 - 0.208 = 1 - R_S$

4.2   Summary

The following steps describe the relationship between structure function of system success/failure with reliability/unreliability and availability/unavailability.

1. Determine the structure function.
2. Express system (un)reliability or (un)availability as a function of component (un)reliabilities or (un)availabilities.
3. Determine component (un)reliabilities or (un)availabilities.

The availability of the product is the fraction of the total test interval that it is performing within specification (up):

$$\text{Availability (A)} = \frac{\text{Total up time}}{\text{Test interval}}$$

$$= \frac{\text{Total up time}}{\text{Total up time} + \text{Total down time}}$$

$$= \frac{N_F \times \text{MTBF}}{N_F \times \text{MTBF} + N_F \times \text{MDT}}$$

$$= \frac{\text{MTBF}}{\text{MTBF} + \text{MDT}} \tag{4.1}$$

Unavailability U is defined as the fraction of the total test interval that it is not performing to specification (failed or down):

$$\text{Unavailability (U)} = \frac{\text{Total down time}}{\text{Test interval}}$$

$$= \frac{\text{MDT}}{\text{MTBF} + \text{MDT}} \tag{4.2}$$

$$\text{Then, A} + \text{U} = 1 \tag{4.3}$$

Availability:

- can be increased by increasing MTBF, i.e. reducing mean failure rate
- depends on MTBF, i.e. depends on reliability
- can be increased by reducing MDT
- depends on MDT, i.e. depends on maintainability (how quickly the product can be repaired and put back into service)

4.3   Availability of Systems with Repair

The steady state availability A_{ss} is the long-term probability that the element is in the up state [5]:

$$A_{ss} = \frac{\mu}{\mu + \lambda} \tag{4.4}$$

Similarly the steady state unavailability U_{ss} is the long-term probability that the element is in the down state:

$$U_{ss} = \frac{\lambda}{\mu + \lambda} \tag{4.5}$$

For a series system consisting of m elements, the system availability is:

$$A_s = A_1 A_2 A_3 \dots A_i \dots A_m \tag{4.6}$$

The unavailability of series system with small U's:

$$U_s = U_1 + U_2 + \dots + U_i + \dots U_m \tag{4.7}$$

For a parallel system of n elements, the system unavailability is given by:

$$U_s = U_1 U_2 U_3 \dots U_j \dots U_n \tag{4.8}$$

For a majority parallel or "k out of n" system, the availability can be calculated using the binomial expansion of $(A + U)^n$.
For "2 out of 4":

$$(A + U)^4 = A^4 + 4A^3 U + 6A^2 U^2 + 4A U^3 + U^4 \tag{4.9}$$

Thus the availability of two or more units is:

$$A_s = A^4 + 4A^3 U + 6A^2 U^2 \tag{4.10}$$

References

1. Rausand, M. and Hoyland, A., *System Reliability Theory: Models, Statistical Methods, and Applications*, John Wiley & Sons, Inc., 2004.
2. Kumamoto, H. and Henley, E.J., *Probabilistic Risk Assessment and Management for Engineers and Scientists*, Second edition, IEEE Press, 1996.
3. Misra, K.B., *Reliability Prediction and Analysis: A Methodology Oriented Treatment*, Elsevier, 1992.
4. Misra, K.B., *New Trends in System Reliability Evaluation*, Elsevier, 1993.
5. Bentley, J., *Introduction to Reliability and Quality Engineering*, Second edition, Pearson, 1999.

5

Data Analysis

5.1   Theoretical Model and Evidence

There are two types of data that can be analyzed from:

Theoretical Model	Evidence
Failure distribution,	Sample,
e.g., $f(t) = \lambda e^{-\lambda t}$	e.g., $\{t_1, \dots, t_n\}$

- How do we estimate λ from the evidence?
- How confident are we in this estimate?
- Two methods can be used:
  - *Classical (frequentist) statistics*
  - *Bayesian statistics*
- The observed values are independent and the underlying distribution is constant.
- Sample mean: $\bar{t} = \dfrac{1}{n} \sum_1^n t_i$

- <u>Sample variance:</u> $s^2 = \dfrac{1}{(n-1)} \sum_{1}^{n} (t_i - \bar{t})^2$

- Set the theoretical moments equal to the sample moments and determine the values of the parameters of the theoretical distribution.

The Method of Moments: Exponential Distribution

- *Exponential distribution:* $\dfrac{1}{\lambda} = \bar{t}$

  Sample: {10.2, 54.0, 23.3, 41.2, 73.2, 28.0} hrs

  $\bar{t} = \dfrac{1}{6}(10.2 + 54 + 23.3 + 41.2 + 73.2 + 28) = \dfrac{229.9}{6} = 38.32$

  $MTTF = 38.32 \quad hrs;$

  $\lambda = \dfrac{1}{38.32} = 0.026 \quad hr^{-1}$

The Method of Moments: Poisson Distribution

- Sample: {r events in t}
- Average number of events: r
- $\lambda t = r \quad \Rightarrow \quad \lambda = \dfrac{r}{t}$
- {3 eqs in 7 years} $\quad \Rightarrow \quad \lambda = \dfrac{3}{7} = 0.43 \quad yr^{-1}$

The Method of Moments: Binomial Distribution

- Sample: {k 1s in n trials}

- Average number of 1s: k

- $qn = k \quad \Rightarrow \quad q = \dfrac{k}{n}$

- {3 failures to start in 17 tests} $q = \dfrac{3}{17} = 0.176$

5.2   Censored Samples

- *Complete sample:*   All n components fail.
- *Censored sample:*   Sampling is terminated at time t_0 (with k failures observed) or when the rth failure occurs.

- Define the *total operational time* as:

$$T = \sum_1^k t_i + (n-k)t_0 \qquad T = \sum_1^r t_i + (n-r)t_r$$

- It can be shown that: $\lambda = \dfrac{k}{T}$ or $\lambda = \dfrac{r}{T}$

- Valid for the exponential distribution <u>only</u> (no memory).

Example

- Sample: 15 components are tested and the test is terminated when the 6th failure occurs.
- The observed failure times are:
  {10.2, 23.3, 28.0, 41.2, 54.0, 73.2} hrs
- The total operational time is:

$$T = 10.2 + 23.3 + 28 + 41.2 + 54 + 73.2 + (15-6)73.2 = 888.7$$

Therefore $\lambda = \dfrac{6}{888.7} = 6.75 x 10^{-3} \quad hr^{-1}$

5.3 Bayesian Theorem

This theorem [1-6] is used to find more accurate estimate of probability (posterior probability).

$$P(H_i/E) = \frac{P(E/H_i)P(H_i)}{\sum_1^N P(E/H_i)P(H_i)}$$

- Prior information can be utilized via the prior distribution.
- Evidence other than statistical can be accommodated via the likelihood function.

Example:
A piece of pipe at a facility may be subjected to a particular aging mechanism. The probability that the mechanism exists is 0.5. A visual inspection has a probability of 0.6 of identifying the mechanism, if it exists, and a probability of 0.1 of declaring that it is there, if it does not exist ("false alarm").

a) What is the probability that the mechanism actually exists, when the visual test is positive?

For this problem, we need to use Bayes' Theorem. First, recall that conditional probability for event A, given event B, is defined as:

$$P\left(A/B\right) \equiv \frac{P\left(AB\right)}{P\left(B\right)}$$

Bayes' Theorem states that:

$$P\left(H_i/E\right) = \frac{P\left(E/H_i\right)P\left(H_i\right)}{\displaystyle\sum_1^N P\left(E/H_i\right)P\left(H_i\right)}$$

In this case, E = the result of the test, which can be either positive or negative,

E$_+$ or E$_-$.

H$_i$ indicates whether of not the pipe aging mechanism exists:

H$_1$ means the mechanisms exists, and
H$_0$ means the mechanisms does *not* exist.

In part (a), we want to calculate P(H$_1$ | E$_+$).
Using Bayes' Theorem:
P(H$_1$ | E$_+$) = [P(E$_+$ | H$_1$) P(H$_1$)] / [P(E$_+$ | H$_1$) P(H$_1$) + P(E$_+$ | H$_0$) P(H$_0$)]

From the problem statement:
"The probability that the mechanism exists is 0.5": P(H$_1$) = 0.5
Since the mechanisms either exists or doesn't, P(H$_0$) = 1 - P(H$_1$) = 0.5
"A visual inspection has a probability of 0.6 of identifying the mechanism, if it exists":
P(E$_+$ | H$_1$) = 0.6
"and a probability of 0.1 of declaring that it is there, if it does not exist":
P(E$_+$ | H$_0$) = 0.1.
Using the Bayes' Theorem above:
P(H$_1$ | E$_+$) = [0.6*0.5] / [0.6*0.5 + 0.1*0.5]
P(H$_1$ | E$_+$) = 0.8571

b)   What is the probability that the mechanism actually exists,

when the visual test is negative?
P(H$_1$ | E$_-$) = [P(E$_-$ | H$_1$) P(H$_1$)] / [P(E$_-$ | H$_1$) P(H$_1$) + P(E$_-$ | H$_0$) P(H$_0$)]
Now we know that a visual inspection has a probability of 0.6 of identifying the mechanism, if it exists; we can calculate the probability of *not* identifying the mechanisms if it exists:
P(E$_-$ | H$_1$) = 1 - P(E$_+$ | H$_1$)
P(E$_-$ | H$_1$) = 1 − 0.6 = 0.4

By the same logic, if the visual inspection has a probability of 0.1 of declaring that it is there, if it does not exist:

$P(E_- | H_0) = 1 - P(E_+ | H_0) = 1 - 0.1 = 0.9$

We have all the information to solve for $P(H_1 | E_-)$:

$P(H_1 | E_-) = [0.4 * 0.5] / [(0.4 * 0.5) + (0.9 * 0.5)]$

$P(H_1 | E_-) = 0.3077$

Summary Table

Statement	Meaning	Implication
The probability that the mechanism exists is 0.5	$P(H_1) = 0.5$	$P(H_0) = 0.5$
A visual inspection has a probability of 0.6 of identifying the mechanism, if it exists	$P(E_+ | H_1) = 0.6$	$P(E_- | H_1) = 0.4$
A visual inspection has a probability of 0.1 of declaring that the mechanism is there, if it does not exist	$P(E_+ | H_0) = 0.1$	$P(E_- | H_0) = 0.9$

References

1. Lewis, E. E., *Introduction to Reliability Engineering*, Second Edition, John Wiley & Sons, Ltd., 1994.
2. O'Connor, P.D.T. and Kleyner, A., *Practical Reliability Engineering*, Fifth Edition, John Wiley & Sons, Ltd., 2012.
3. Walpole, R.E., Myers, R.H., and Myers, S.L., *Probability and Statistics for Engineers and Scientists*, Sixth edition, Prentice Hall, 1998.
4. Montgomery, D.C. and Runger, G.C., *Applied Statistics and Probability for Engineers*, Second edition, John Wiley & Sons, Inc., 1999.
5. Ross, S.M., *Introduction to Probability Models*, Sixth edition, Academic Press, 1999.
6. Montgomery, D.C., Runger, G.C., and Hubele, N.F., *Engineering Statistics*, John Wiley & Sons, Inc., 1998.

6

Introduction to Network Systems

A computer network system plays an important role in the transmission of information. It is basically a collection of interconnected computers that provide interprocess communication. The transferring or exchanging information is transmitted via networks in packets (short messages), which contain information and user data. The length of each packet is limited by a maximum length determined by the network.

There is an increasing demand for computer networks since they provide an economical means of sharing computers resources, such as hardware, software, and databases. Besides that, several advantages of computer networks are: to improve reliability of networks through backup and redundancy, to manage distribution of processing functions, to supply centralized management and allocation of network resources, and to provide network users with maximum performance at minimum cost.

There are three main categories of computer networks: local, wide, and metropolitan area networks. Local Area Networks, generally called LANs, are privately-owned networks within a single building or campus of up to a few kilometers in size. They are widely used to connect personal computers and workstations in company offices and factories to share resources (e.g., printers) and exchange information. LANs are distinguished from other kinds of networks by three characteristics: size, transmission technology, and topology. A Metropolitan Area Network or MAN is a bigger version of a LAN and normally uses similar technology. It might cover a group of nearby corporate offices or a city and might be either private or public. A MAN can support both data and voice, and might even be related to the local cable television network. Wide Area Networks (WANs) span a large geographical area, often a country or continent. They contain a collection of machines intended for running user (i.e., application) programs.

The demand for even more computing power has never stopped. A number of important problems have been identified in the areas of defense, aerospace, automotive applications, weather forecasting, map making, aerodynamic simulations, chemical reaction simulations, seismic data processing, air traffic control, robot vision, and science, whose solution requires tremendous amount of computational power. There are fundamental considerations as speed of computer device reaches a limit and an execution rate required simply beyond the capabilities of current large computer systems. Hence, these facts result that the system performance in the future can only significantly increased through additional concurrent processing. As a result, parallel computers with multiple processors can supply the support essential to meeting the computational performance goals for all these applications. The means for communication among processors, memory modules, and other devices of a parallel computer is the interconnection network.

Interconnection networks are a natural result of advances in computer technology that provide the need in the improved system performance. As computer systems evolved, the hardware costs being a significant limiting factor. However, interconnection technology is creating an entirely new atmosphere; it is now economically feasible to construct a multiple-processor computer system by interconnecting a large number of processors and memory modules. Interconnection networks are currently being used for many different applications such as telephone switches, processor/memory interconnects for supercomputer, networks for industrial application, and wide area computer networks. Therefore, concept, design, and implementation of interconnection networks are crucial factors at this point in time.

6.1   Parallel Computing and Networks

In general, a parallel processing system is a computer system consisting of a control unit, N processors, N memory modules, and an interconnection network. The interconnection network is bi-directional if it connects each processor to all or some subset of memories, as well as each memory to all or some subset of processors. A transfer instruction results in data being moved from each processor to one or more of the memories to which that processor is connected by the network, or from each memory to one or more of the processors to which that memory is connected by the network. One processor can transfer data to another processor through any memory to which both are connected. To pass data between two processors, a programmed sequence of data transfer must be executed. This sequence of transfers moves the data from one processor to the other by passing the data through intermediary memories (and possibly processors).

A major problem in designing large-scale parallel/distributed systems is the construction of an interconnection network to provide interprocessor communications and in some cases, memory access for the processors. The task of interconnecting N processors and N memory modules, where N may be in the range of 2^6 to 2^{16}, is not trivial. The interconnection scheme must provide fast and flexible communications at a reasonable cost. A single shared bus, as shown in Figure 6.1, is not sufficient, because it is often desirable to allow all processors to send data to other processors simultaneously. Ideally, each processor should be linked directly to every other processor so that the system is completely connected, as shown for N = 8 in Figure 6.2.

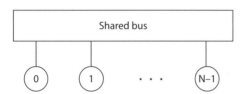

Figure 6.1 A Single Shared Bus Providing Communications for N Devices.

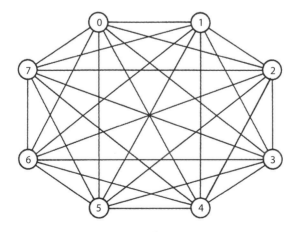

Figure 6.2 A Completely Connected System for N = 8.

In this example, it could be assumed that each node is a processor with its own memory, or those even numbered nodes are processors and odd numbered nodes are memories. Unfortunately, these configurations are highly impractical when N is large because N – 1 unidirectional lines are required for each processor.

An alternative interconnection scheme that allows all processors to communicate simultaneously is the cross bar network shown in Figure 6.3. In this example, the processors communicate through the memories. The network may be viewed as a set of intersecting lines, where interconnections between processors and memories are specified by the crosspoint switches at each line intersection [1]. The difficulty with crossbar networks is that N^2 crosspoint switches are needed. Therefore, the cost of the network grows with N^2, which, given current technology, makes it infeasible for large systems.

To solve a problem of providing fast, efficient communications at a reasonable cost, many different networks between the extremes of the single bus and the completely connected scheme have been proposed in the literature. There is no single network that is generally considered best. The cost effectiveness of a particular network design depends on such factors as the computational tasks for which it will be used, the desired speed of interprocessor data transfers, the actual hardware requirement for a network, the number of processors in the system, and any cost constraints on the construction.

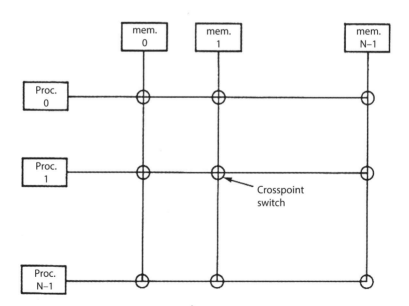

Figure 6.3 A Crossbar Network Connecting N Processors to N Memories.

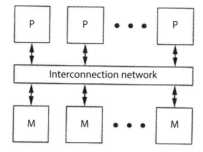

Figure 6.4 Hardware Model of Concurrent Processing System.

This chapter is an in depth study of a collection of network designs that can be used to support large scale parallelism. These networks can provide the communications needed in a parallel processing system consisting of a large number of processors (in the 2^6 to 2^{16} range, for example) that are working together to perform a single overall task. Many of these networks can be used in dynamically reconfigurable machines that can perform independent multiple tasks, where each task is processed using parallelism. A general model of the hardware system is shown in Figure 6.4. This hardware model consists of a set of processors, a set of memory, and an interconnection network between processors and memory. The interconnection network facilitates communication not only among the processors and the memory modules but also between the processors and memory modules. In this case, shared-memory multiprocessors model simplifies the task of exchanging data among processors.

6.2   Network Design Considerations

Interconnection networks play a major role in the performance of modern parallel computers. There are many factors that may affect the choice of an appropriate interconnection network for the underlying parallel computing platform [2]. These factors include:

1. *Performance requirements.* Processes executing in different processors synchronize and communicate through the interconnection network. These operations are usually performed by explicit message passing or by accessing shared variables. Message latency is the time elapsed between the time a message is generated at its source node and the time

the message is delivered at its destination node. Message latency directly affects processor idle time and memory access time to remote memory locations. Also, the network may saturate, it may be unable to deliver the flow of messages injected by the nodes, limiting the effective computing power of a parallel computer. The maximum amount of information delivered by the network per time unit defines the throughput of that network.

2. *Scalability*. A scalable architecture implies that as more processors are added, their memory bandwidth, I/O bandwidth, and network bandwidth should increase proportionally. Otherwise, the components whose bandwidth does not scale may become a bottleneck for the rest of the system, decreasing the overall efficiency accordingly.

3. *Incremental expandability*. Customers are unlikely to purchase a parallel computer with a full set of processors and memories. As the budget permits, more processors and memories may be added until a system's maximum configuration is reached. In some interconnection networks, the number of processors must be a power of 2, which makes them difficult to expand. In other cases, expandability is provided at the cost of wasting resources. For example, a network designed for a maximum size of 1,024 nodes may contain many unused communication links when the network is implemented with a smaller size. Interconnection networks should provide incremental expandability, allowing the addition of a small number of nodes while minimizing resource wasting.

4. *Partitionability*. Several users usually share parallel computers at a time. In this case, it is desirable that the network traffic produced by each user does not affect the performance of other applications. This can be ensured if the network can be partitioned into smaller functional subsystems. Partitionability may also be required for security reasons.

5. *Simplicity*. Simple designs often lead to higher clock frequencies and may achieve higher performance. Additionally, customers appreciate networks that are easy to understand because it is easier to exploit their performance.

6. *Distance span*. This factor may lead to very different implementations. In multicomputers and distributed shared memory multiprocessors, the network is assembled inside

a few cabinets. The maximum distance between nodes is small. As a consequence, signals are usually transmitted using copper wires. These wires can be arranged regularly, reducing the computer size and wire length. In networks of workstations, links have very different lengths and some links may be very long, producing problems such as electromagnetic noise and heavy link cables. The use of optical links solve these problems, equalizing the bandwidth of short and long links up to a much greater distance than when copper wire is used. Also, geographical constraints may impose the use of irregular connection patterns between nodes, making distributed control more difficult to implement.

7. *Physical constraints.* An interconnection network connects processors, memories, and/or I/O devices. It is desirable for a network to accommodate a large number of components while maintaining low communication latency. As the number of components increases, the number of wires needed to interconnect them also increases. Packaging these components together usually requires meeting certain physical constraints, such as operating temperature control, wiring length limitation, and space limitation. Two major implementation problems in large networks are the arrangement of wires in a limited area and the number of pins per chip (or board) dedicated to communication channels. In other words, the complexity of the connection is limited by the maximum wire density possible, and by the maximum pin count. The speed at which a machine can run is limited by the wire lengths, and the majority of the power consumed by the system is used to drive the wires. This is an important and challenging issue to be considered. Different engineering technologies for packaging, wiring, and maintenance should be considered.

8. *Reliability and maintainability.* An interconnection network should be able to deliver information reliably. Interconnection networks can be designed for continuous operation in the presence of a limited number of faults. These networks should be able to send messages through alternative paths when some faults are detected. In this case, performance and fault tolerance are two dominant issues facing the design of interconnection networks for

large-scale multiprocessors architectures. Fault tolerance is the ability of the network to function in the presence of component failures. In addition to reliability, interconnection networks should have a modular design, allowing hot upgrades and repairs. Nodes can also fail or be removed from the network. In particular, a node can be powered off (not operational) in a network of workstations. Thus, networks of workstations usually require some reconfiguration algorithm for the automatic reconfiguration of the network when a node is powered on (functional) or off (not operational). Typically, detection mechanisms are assumed to have identified one of two classes of faults, either the entire processing element (PE) can fail, or any communication channel may fail. The former is referred to as a node failure and the latter as a link failure. On a node failure, all physical links incident on the failed node are marked faulty. When a physical link fails, then all virtual channels on that particular physical link are marked faulty. Note that many types of failures will simply manifest themselves as link or node failures. For example, the failure of the link controller, or the virtual channel buffers, appear as a link failure. On the other hand, the failure of the router control unit or the associated PE effectively appears as a node failure.

9. *Expected workloads.* Users of a general-purpose machine may have very different requirements. If the kind of applications that will be executed in the parallel computer are known in advance, it may be possible to extract some information on usual communication patterns, message sizes, network load, etc. That information can be used for the optimization of some design parameters. When it is not possible to get information on expected workloads, network design should be robust, i.e. design parameters should be selected in such a way that performance is good over a wide range of traffic conditions.

10. *Cost constraints.* Finally, it is obvious that the "best" network may be too expensive. Design decisions very often are trade-off between cost and other design factors. Fortunately, cost is not always directly proportional to performance. Using commodity components whenever possible may considerably reduce the overall cost.

6.3   Classification of Interconnection Networks

Interconnection networks have been traditionally classified according to four design decisions [3]: operation mode, control strategy, switching methodology, and network topology.

1. *Operation Mode.* Two types of communication can be identified: synchronous and asynchronous. Synchronous communication is needed for processing in which communication paths are established synchronously for either a data manipulating function or a data/instruction broadcast. Asynchronous communication is needed for multiprocessing in which connection requests are issued dynamically. A system may also be designed to facilitate both synchronous and asynchronous processing. Therefore, typical operation modes of interconnection networks can be classified into three categories: synchronous, asynchronous, and combined.

2. *Control strategy.* A typical interconnection network consists of a number of switching elements and interconnection links. Interconnection functions are realized by properly setting control of the switching elements. The control-setting function can be managed by a centralized controller or by the individual switching element. The latter strategy is called distributed control and the first strategy is called centralized control.

3. *Switching methodology.* The two major switching methodologies are circuit switching and packet switching. In circuit switching, a physical path is actually established between a source and a destination. In packet switching, data is put in a packet and routed through the interconnection network without establishing a physical connection path. In general, circuit switching is much more suitable for bulk data transmission, and packet switching is more efficient for short data messages. Another option, integrated switching, includes capabilities of both circuit switching and packet switching. Therefore, three switching methodologies can be identified: circuit switching, packet switching, and integrated switching.

4. *Network topology.* A network can be depicted by a graph in which nodes represent switching points and edges represent communication links. The topologies tend to be regular and

can be grouped into two categories: static and dynamic. In a static topology, links between two processors are passive and dedicated buses cannot be reconfigured for direct connections to other processors. On the other hand, links in the dynamic category can be reconfigured by setting the network's active switching elements.

The cross product of the set of categories in each design decision: {operation mode} x {control strategy} x {switching methodology} x {network topology} represents a *space of interconnection networks*. Obviously, the cross product contains some uninteresting cases, but a network designer can obtain a meaningful subspace by exercising a practical view of engineering technology.

A classification scheme is shown in Figure 6.5 which categorizes the known interconnection networks into four major classes based primarily on network topology: shared-medium networks, direct networks, indirect networks, and hybrid networks. For each class, the figure shows a hierarchy of subclasses, also indicating some real implementations for most of them. This classification scheme is based on the classification proposed in [4], and it mainly focuses on networks that have been implemented. It is by no means complete as other new and innovative interconnection networks may emerge as technology further advances, such as mobile communication and optical interconnections.

In shared-medium networks, the transmission medium is shared by all communicating devices. An alternative to this approach consists of having point-to-point links directly connecting each communicating device to a (usually small) subset of other communicating devices in the networks. In this case, any communication between non-neighboring devices requires transmitting the information through several intermediate devices. These networks are known as direct networks. Instead of directly connecting the communicating devices among them, indirect networks connect those devices by means of one or more switches. If several switches exist, they are connected among them using point-to-point links. In this case, any communication among communicating devices requires transmitting the information through one or more switches. Finally, hybrid approaches are possible. These networks classes and the corresponding subclasses will be described in the following sections.

(1-D = one-dimensional; 2-D = two-dimensional; 3-D = three dimensional; CMU = Carnegie Mellon University; DASH = Directory Architecture for Shared-Memory; DEC = Digital Equipment Corp.; FDDI = Fiber Distributed Data Interface; HP = Hewlett-Packard; KSR = Kendall Square

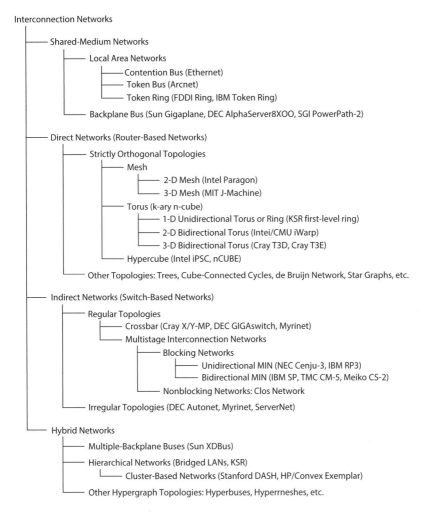

Figure 6.5 Classification of Interconnection Networks.

Research; MIN = Multistage Interconnection Network; MIT = Massachusetts Institute of Technology; SGI = Silicon Graphics Inc.; TMC = Thinking Machine Corp.)

6.3.1 Shared-Medium Networks

The least complex interconnect structure is one in which the transmission medium is shared by all communicating devices. In such shared-medium networks, only one device is allowed to use the network at a time. Every device attached to the network has requester, driver, and receiver circuits to handle the passing of address and data. The network itself is usually passive, since the network itself does not generate messages.

An important issue here is the arbitration strategy that determines the mastership of the shared-medium network to resolve network access conflicts. A unique characteristic of a shared medium is its ability to have broadcast capability; in which all devices on the medium can monitor network activities and receive the information transmitted on the shared medium. This property is important to efficiently support many applications requiring one-to-all or one-to-many communication services, such as barrier synchronization and snoopy cache coherence protocols. Due to limited network bandwidth, a single shared medium can only support limited number of devices before the medium becomes a bottleneck.

Shared-medium networks constitute a well-established technology. Additionally, their limited bandwidth restricts their use in multiprocessors. There are two major classes of shared-medium networks: local area networks, mainly used to construct computer networks that span physical distances no longer than a few kilometers, and backplane buses, mainly used for internal communication in uniprocessors and multiprocessors.

Shared-Medium Local Area Networks. High-speed LANs can be used as a networking backbone to interconnect computers to provide an integrated parallel and distributed computing environment. Physically, a shared-medium LAN uses copper wires or fiber optics in a bit-serial fashion as the transmission medium. The network topology is either a bus or a ring (a natural extension of a single-bus network as the passing of the data forms a ring structure). Depending on the arbitration mechanism used, different LANs have been commercially available. For performance and implementation reasons, it is impractical to have a centralized control or to have some fixed access assignment to determine the bus master who can access the bus. The major classes of LANs based on distributed control are contention bus, token bus, and token ring.

Shared-Medium Backplane Bus. A backplane bus is the simplest interconnection structure for bus-based parallel computers. It is commonly used to interconnect processor(s) and memory modules to provide uniform memory access architecture. A typical backplane bus usually has 50 – 300 wires and is physically realized by printed lines on a circuit board or by discrete (backplane) wiring. Additional costs are incurred by interface electronics, such as line drivers, receivers, and connectors.

There are three kinds of information in the backplane bus: data, address, and control signals. Control signals include bus request signal and request grant signal, among many others. In addition of the width of data lines, the maximum bus bandwidth that can be provided is dependent on the technology. The number of processors that can be put on a bus depends on many factors, such as processor speed, bus bandwidth, cache architecture, and program behavior.

6.3.2   Direct Networks

Scalability is an important issue in designing multiprocessor systems. Bus-based systems are not scalable, as the bus becomes the bottleneck when more processors are added. The direct network or point-to-point network is a popular network architecture that scales well to a large number of processors. A direct network consists of a set of nodes, each one being directly connected to a (usually small) subset of other nodes in the network. The corresponding interconnection patterns between nodes will be discussed below. Each node is a programmable computer with its own processor, local memory, and other supporting devices. These nodes may have different functional capabilities. For example, the set of nodes may contain vector processors, graphics processors, and I/O processors. Figure 6.6 shows the architecture of a generic node. A common component of these nodes is a router, which handles message communication among nodes. For this reason, direct networks are also known as router-based networks. Each router has direct connections to the router of its neighbors. Usually, two neighboring nodes are connected by a pair of unidirectional channels in opposite directions. A bidirectional channel may also be used to connect two neighboring nodes. Although the function of a router can be performed by the local processor, dedicated routers have been used in high-performance multicomputers, allowing overlapped computation and communication within each node. As the number of nodes in the system

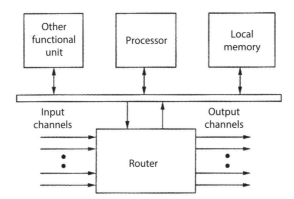

Figure 6.6 A Generic Node Architecture.

increases, the total communication bandwidth, memory bandwidth, and processing capability of the system also increase. Thus, direct networks have been a popular interconnection architecture for constructing large-scale parallel computers.

Each router supports some number of input and output channels. Internal channels or ports connect the local processor/memory to the router. Although it is common to provide only one pair of internal channels, some systems use more internal channels in order to avoid a communication bottleneck between the local processor/memory and the router. External channels are used for communication between routers. By connecting input channels of one node to the output channels of other nodes, the direct network is defined. Unless otherwise specified, the term channel will refer to an external channel. Two directly connected nodes are called neighboring or adjacent nodes. Usually, each node has a fixed number of input and output channels, and every input channel is paired with a corresponding output channel. Through the connections among these channels, there are many ways to interconnect these nodes. Obviously, every node in the network should be able to reach every other node.

Direct networks have been traditionally modeled by a graph G(N, C), where the vertices of the graph N represent the set of processing nodes, and the edges of the graph C represent the set of communication channels. This is a very simple model that does not consider implementation issues. However, it allows the study of many interesting network properties. Depending on the properties under study, a bidirectional channel may be modeled either as an edge or as two arcs in opposite directions (two unidirectional channels). Let us assume that a bidirectional channel is modeled as an edge. Some basic network properties can be defined from the graph representation: node degree (number of channels connecting that node to its neighbors), diameter (the maximum distance between two nodes in the network), regularity (a network is regular when all the nodes have the same degree), and symmetry (a network is symmetric when it looks alike from every node).

A direct network is mainly characterized by three factors: topology, routing, and switching. The topology defines how the nodes are interconnected by channels and is usually modeled by a graph as indicated above. For direct networks, the ideal topology would connect every node to every other node. No message would even have to pass through an intermediate node before reaching its destination. This fully connected topology requires a router with N links (including the internal one) for a network with N nodes. Therefore, the cost is prohibitive for networks of moderate to large size. Additionally, the number of physical connections of a node is limited by hardware constraints such as the number of available pins and the available wiring area. These engineering and scaling difficulties preclude the use of such fully connected networks even for small network sizes. As a consequence, many topologies have been proposed, trying to balance performance and some cost parameters. In these topologies, messages may have to traverse some intermediate nodes before reaching the destination node.

Many network topologies have been proposed in terms of their graph theoretic properties. However, very few of them have ever been implemented. Most of the implemented networks have an orthogonal topology. A network topology is orthogonal if and only if nodes can be arranged in an orthogonal n-dimensional space, and every link can be arranged in such a way that it produces a displacement in a single dimension. Figures 6.7 through 6.9 show several direct networks.

Orthogonal topologies can be further classified as strictly orthogonal and weakly orthogonal. In a strictly orthogonal topology, every node has at least one link crossing each dimension. In a weakly orthogonal topology, some nodes may not have any link in some dimensions. Hence, it is not possible to cross every dimension from every node. Crossing a given dimension from a given node may require moving in another

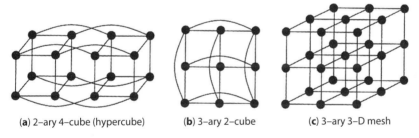

| (**a**) 2–ary 4–cube (hypercube) | (**b**) 3–ary 2–cube | (**c**) 3–ary 3–D mesh |

Figure 6.7 Strictly Orthogonal Direct Network Topologies.

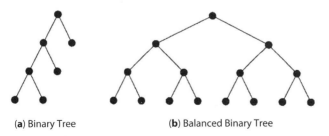

| (**a**) Binary Tree | (**b**) Balanced Binary Tree |

Figure 6.8 Some Tree Topologies.

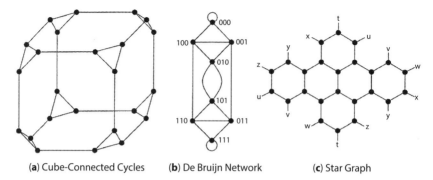

(a) Cube-Connected Cycles   (b) De Bruijn Network   (c) Star Graph

Figure 6.9 Other Direct Network Topologies.

dimension first. The most popular strictly orthogonal topologies are the n-dimensional mesh, the k-ary n-cube or torus, and the hypercube. The other topologies include: trees, cube-connected cycles, de Bruijn network, and star graphs.

6.3.3 Indirect Networks

Indirect or switch-based networks are another major class of interconnection networks. Instead of providing a direct connection among some nodes, the communication between any two nodes has to be carried through some switches. Each node has a network adapter that connects to a network switch. Each switch can have a set of ports. Each port consists of one input and one output link. A (possibly empty) set of ports in each switch are either connected to processors or left open, whereas the remaining ports are connected to ports of other switches to provide connectivity between the processor. The interconnection of those switches defines various network topologies.

Switch-based networks considerably evolved over time. A wide range of topologies have been proposed, ranging from regular topologies used in array processors and shared- memory uniform memory access multiprocessors to the irregular topologies currently used in network of workstations. Regular topologies have regular connection patterns between switches while irregular topologies do not follow any predefined pattern. Regular topologies include the crossbar and the multistage interconnection network. Figure 6.10 shows a typical switch-based network with irregular topology. Both network classes can be further classified according to the number of switches a message has to traverse before reaching its destination. Although this classification is not important in

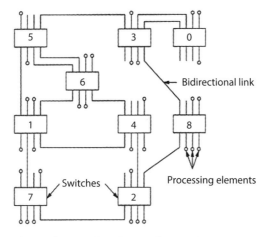

Figure 6.10 A Switch-Based Network with Irregular Topology.

the case of irregular topologies, it makes a big difference in the case of regular networks because some specific properties can be derived for each network class.

Indirect networks can also be modeled by a graph G(N, C), where N is the set of switches, and C is the set of unidirectional or bidirectional links between the switches. For the analysis of most properties, it is not necessary to explicitly include processing nodes in the graph. Although a similar model can be used for direct and indirect networks, a few differences exist between them. Each switch in an indirect network may be connected to zero, one, or more processors. Obviously, only the switches connected to some processors can be the source or the destination of a message. Additionally, transmitting a message from a node to another node requires crossing the link between the source node and the switch connected to it, and the link between the last switch in the path and the destination node.

Similar to direct networks, an indirect network is mainly characterized by three factors: topology, routing, and switching. The topology defines how the switches are interconnected by channels. For indirect networks with N nodes, the ideal topology would connect those nodes through a single N x N switches. Such a switch is known as a crossbar. Although using a single N x N crossbar is much cheaper than using a fully directed direct network topology (requiring N routers, each one having an internal N x N crossbar), the cost is still prohibitive for large networks. Similar to direct networks, the number of physical connections of a switch is limited by hardware constraints such as the number of available pins and the available wiring area. These engineering and scaling difficulties preclude the use of crossbar networks for large network sizes. As a consequence, many alternative topologies have been proposed. In these topologies, messages may have to traverse several switches before reaching the destination node. In regular networks, these switches are usually identical and have been traditionally organized as a set of stages. Each stage (but the input/output stages) is only connected to the previous and next stages using regular connection patterns. Input/output stages are connected to the nodes as well as to another stage in the network. These networks are referred to as multistage networks, and have different properties depending on the number of stages, and how those stages are arranged. The classification of the multistage interconnection networks includes the topology of the networks, switching elements sizes used, and all the properties of those networks will be discussed in chapter 7.

6.3.4   Hybrid Networks

In general, hybrid networks combine mechanisms from shared-medium networks and direct or indirect networks. Therefore, they increase bandwidth with respect to shared-medium networks, and reduce the distance between nodes with respect to direct and indirect networks. However, for systems requiring very high performance, direct and indirect networks achieve better scalability than hybrid networks because point-to-point links are simpler and faster than shared-medium buses. Recently hybrid networks have been gaining acceptance again. The use of optical technology enables the implementation of high performance buses.

Many hybrid networks have been proposed for different purposes. In general, hybrid networks can be modeled by a hypergraph [5], where the vertices of the hypergraph represent the set of processing nodes, and the edges represent the set of communication channels and/or buses. Note that an edge in a hypergraph can interconnect an arbitrary number of nodes. When an edge connects exactly two nodes then it represents a point-to-point channel. Otherwise, it represents a bus. In some network designs, each bus has a single driving node. No other device is allowed to drive that bus. In this case, there is no need for arbitration. Hybrid networks include the multiple backplane buses, hierarchical networks, cluster-based networks, and other hypergraph topologies. One interesting class of the other hypergraph topologies is the hypermesh, which is a regular topology consisting of a set of nodes arranged into several dimensions. Instead of having direct connections to the neighbors in each dimension, each node is connected to all the nodes in each dimension through a bus. Figures 6.11 through 6.14 show several hybrid networks.

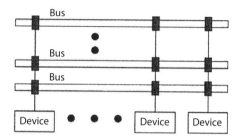

Figure 6.11 A Multiple-Bus Network.

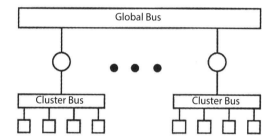

Figure 6.12 Two-Level Hierarchical Buses.

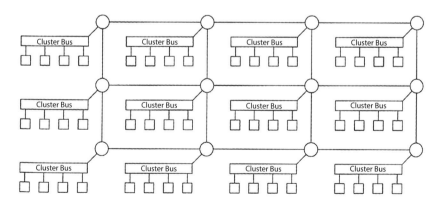

Figure 6.13 Cluster-Based 2-D Mesh.

Figure 6.14 A Two-Dimensional Hypermesh.

References

1. Thurber, K. J., Parallel Processor Architectures – Part 1: General Purpose Systems, *Computer Design*, vol. 18, 89–97, January 1979.
2. Duato, J., Yalmanchili, S., and Ni, L. M., *Interconnection Networks an Engineering Approach*, IEEE Computer Society, Los Alamitos, CA, 1997.
3. Feng, T. Y., A Survey of Interconnection Networks, *Computer*, 12–27, December 1981.
4. Ni, L. M., Issues in Designing Truly Scalable Interconnection Networks, *Proceedings of the 1996 ICPP Workshop on Challenges for Parallel Processing*, 74–83, August 1996.
5. Berge, C., *Graphs and Hypergraphs*, North-Holland, 1973.

7

Classification of Multistage Interconnection Networks

7.1 Background

Multistage Interconnection Networks (MINs) connect input devices to output devices through a number of switch stages, where each switch is a crossbar network. The number of stages and the connection patterns between stages determine the routing capability of the networks. MINs were initially proposed for telephone networks and later for array processors. In these cases, a central controller establishes the path from input to output. In cases where the number of inputs equals the number of outputs, each input synchronously transmits a message to one output, and each output receives a message from exactly one input. Such unicast communication patterns can be represented as a permutation of the input addresses. For this application, MINs have been popular as alignment networks for storing and accessing arrays in parallel from memory banks. Array storage is typically skewed to permit conflict-free access, and the network is used to unscramble the arrays during access. These networks can also be configured with the number of inputs greater than the number of outputs and vice versa. On the other hand, in asynchronous multiprocessors, centralized control and permutation routing are infeasible. In this case, a routing algorithm is required to establish the path across the stages of a MIN.

Depending on the availability of paths to establish new connections, MINs have been traditionally divided into three classes [1]:

1. *Blocking.* A connection between a free input/output pair is not always possible because of conflicts with the existing connections. Typically, there is a unique path between every input/output pair, thus minimizing the number of switches and stages. However, it is also possible to provide multiple paths to reduce conflicts and increase fault tolerance. These blocking networks are also known as multipath.

2. *Nonblocking.* Any input port can be connected to any free output port without affecting the existing connections. Nonblocking networks have the same functionality as a crossbar. They require multiple paths between every input and output, which in turn leads to extra stages.

3. *Rearrangeable.* Any input port can be connected to any free output port. However, the existing connections may require rearrangement of paths. These networks also require multiple paths between every input and output but the number of paths and the cost is smaller than in the case of nonblocking networks.

Nonblocking networks are expensive. Although they are cheaper than a crossbar of the same size, their cost is prohibitive for large sizes. The best-known example of nonblocking multistage network is initially proposed for telephone networks. Rearrangeable networks require less stages or simpler switches than a nonblocking network. Rearrangeable networks require a central controller to rearrange connections, and were proposed for array processors. However, connections cannot be easily rearranged on multiprocessors because processors access the network asynchronously. Therefore, rearrangeable networks behave like blocking networks when accesses are asynchronous.

Depending on the kind of channels and switches, MINs can be split into two classes [2]:

1. *Unidirectional MINs.* Channels and switches are unidirectional.
2. *Bidirectional MINs.* Channels and switches are bidirectional. This implies that information can be transmitted

simultaneously in opposite directions between neighboring switches.

Additionally, each channel may be either multiplexed or replaced by two or more channels. In the latter case, the network is referred to as dilated MIN. Obviously, the number of ports of each switch must increase accordingly.

7.1.1   Unidirectional Multistage Interconnection Networks

The basic building blocks of unidirectional MINs are unidirectional switches. An a × b switch is a crossbar network with a inputs and b outputs. If each input port is allowed to connect to exactly one output port, at most min {a, b} connections can be supported simultaneously. If each input port is allowed to connect to many output ports, a more complicated design is needed to support the one-to-many or multicast communication. In the broadcast mode or one-to-all communication, each input port is allowed to connect to all output ports. Figure 7.1 shows four possible states of a 2 x 2 switch. The last two states are used to support one-to-many and one-to-all communications.

In MINs with N inputs = M outputs, it is common to use switches with the same number of input and output ports, i.e., a = b. If N > M, switches with a > b will be used. Such switches are also called concentration switches. In the case of N < M, distribution switches with a < b will be used.

It can be shown that with N input and output ports, a unidirectional MIN with k × k switches requires at least $\log_k$ N stages to allow a connection path between any input port and any output port. By having additional stages, more connection paths may be used to deliver a message between an input port and an output port at the expense of extra hardware cost. Every path through the MIN crosses all the stages. Therefore, all the paths have the same length.

In general, the topological equivalence of MINs can be viewed as follows: Consider that each input link to the first stage is numbered using

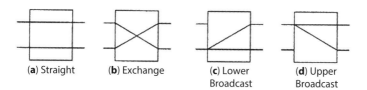

(a) Straight   (b) Exchange   (c) Lower   (d) Upper
                                  Broadcast   Broadcast

Figure 7.1 Four Possible States of a 2 x 2 Switch.

a string of n digits $s_{n-1}s_{n-2}...s_1s_0$, where $0 \le s_i \le k-1$, for $0 \le i \le n-1$. The least significant digit s_0 gives the address of the input port at the corresponding switch and the address of the switch is given by $s_{n-1}s_{n-2}...s_1$. At each stage, a given switch is able to connect any input port with any output port. This can be viewed as changing the value of the least significant digit of the address. In order to be able to connect any input to any output of the network, it should be possible to change the value of all the digits. As each switch is only able to change the value of the least significant digit of the address, connection patterns between stages are defined in such a way that the position of digits is permuted, and after n stages all the digits have occupied the least significant position.

7.1.2   Bidirectional Multistage Interconnection Networks

A bidirectional switch supports three types of connections: forward, backward, and turnaround. Figure 7.2 illustrates a bidirectional switch in which each port is associated with a pair of unidirectional channels in opposite directions. This implies that information can be transmitted simultaneously in opposite directions between neighboring switches. As turnaround connections between ports at the same side of a switch are possible, paths have different lengths. An eight-node butterfly bidirectional MIN (BMIN) is illustrated in Figure 7.3. For ease of explanation, it is assumed that processor nodes are on the left-hand side of the network.

Paths are established in BMINs by crossing stages in forward direction, then establishing a turnaround connection, and finally crossing stages in backward direction. This is usually referred to as turnaround routing. Figure 7.4 shows two alternative paths from node S to node D in an eight-node butterfly BMIN. When crossing stages in forward direction, several paths are possible. Each switch can select any of its output ports. However, once the turnaround connection is crossed, a single path is available up to the destination node. In the worst case, establishing a path in an n-stage BMIN requires crossing 2n − 1 stages.

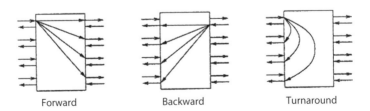

Forward   Backward   Turnaround

Figure 7.2 Connections in a Bidirectional Switch.

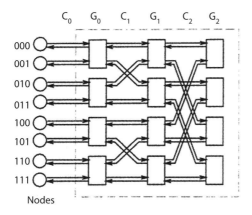

Figure 7.3 An Eight-Node Butterfly Bidirectional MIN.

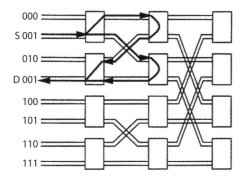

Figure 7.4 Alternative Paths in an Eight-Node Butterfly Bidirectional MIN.

7.1.3   Architectural Models of Parallel Machines

There are a variety of ways to organize the processors, memories, and inter-connection network in a large-scale parallel processing system. In this section, models of a few of the basic structures are briefly introduced [3]:

1. *SIMD Systems.* A model of an *SIMD* (*single instruction stream – multiple data stream*) *system* consists of a control unit, N processors, N memory modules, and an interconnection network. The control unit broadcasts instructions to the processors, and all active processors execute the same instruction at the same time. Thus there is a single instruction stream. Each active processor executes the instruction on data in its own associated memory module. Thus there are multiple data streams. The interconnection network,

sometimes referred to as an alignment or permutation network, provides for communications among the processors and memory modules.

2. *Multiple-SIMD Systems.* A variation on the SIMD model that may permit more efficient use of the system processors and memories is the *multiple-SIMD system*, a parallel processing system that can be dynamically reconfigured to operate as one or more independent SIMD subsystems of various sizes. A multiple-SIMD system consists of N processors, N memory modules, an interconnection network, and C control units, where C < N. Each of the multiple control units can be connected to some disjoint subset of the processors, which communicate over subnetworks, creating independent SIMD subsystems of various sizes.

3. *MIMD Systems.* In contrast to the SIMD system, where all processors follow a single instruction stream, the processors in a parallel system may each follow its own instruction stream, forming an *MIMD (multiple instruction stream – multiple data stream) system.* One organization for an MIMD system consists of N processors, N memory modules, and an interconnection network, where each of the processors executes its own program on its own data. Thus there are multiple instruction streams and multiple data streams. The interconnection network provides communications among the processors and memory modules. While in an SIMD system all active processors use the interconnection network at the same time (i.e., synchronously), in an MIMD system, because each processor is executing its own program, inputs to the network arrive independently (i.e., asynchronously).

4. *Partitionable SIMD/MIMD Systems.* A fourth model of system organization combines the features of the previous three. A *partitionable SIMD/MIMD system* is a parallel processing system that can be dynamically reconfigured to operate as one or more independent SIMD and/or MIMD subsystems of various sizes. The N processors, N memory modules, interconnection network, and C control units of a partitionable SIMD/MIMD system can be partitioned to form independent subsystems as with multiple-SIMD systems. Furthermore, each processor can follow its own instructions (MIMD operation) in addition to being capable of accepting an instruction stream from a control unit (SIMD operation).

Thus each subsystem can operate in the SIMD mode or the MIMD mode. The processors can switch between the two modes of parallelism from one instruction to the next when performing a task, depending on which is more desirable at the time.

5. *System Configurations.* With any of these four models, there are two basic system configurations. One is the *PE-to-PE configuration*, in which each processing element or *PE* (formed by pairing a processor with a local memory) is attached to both an input port and an output port of an interconnection network (i.e., PE j is connected to input port j and output port j). This is also referred to as distributed memory system or private memory system. In contrast, in the *processor-to-memory configuration* processors are attached to one side of an interconnection network and memories are attached to the other side. Processors communicate through shared memories. This is also referred to as a global memory system. Hybrids of the two approaches are also possible, such as using a local cache in a processor-to-memory system. Which configuration or hybrid of them is "best" for a particular system design is a function of many factors, such as the types of computational tasks for which the system is intended (e.g., are most data and/or programs shared by all processors or local to each processor), the operating system philosophy (e.g., will multitasking be done within each processor to hide any latency time for network transfer delays when fetching data), and the characteristics of the processors and memories to be used (e.g., clock speed, availability of cache). Beware of the term *shared memory* as applied to these parallel systems. Some researchers use this term to refer to the way in which a system is physically constructed (i.e., processor-to-memory configuration) and others use it to refer to the logical addressing method.

7.1.4   Terminology

Many interconnection networks for large-scale multiprocessor computer systems have been proposed. Of these, Multistage Interconnection Networks (MINs) offer a good balance between cost and performance. In this section, the common terminologies in MINs such as switches, links, ports, crossbar, fault-tolerant, topology, routing tag, path, and connection are discussed.

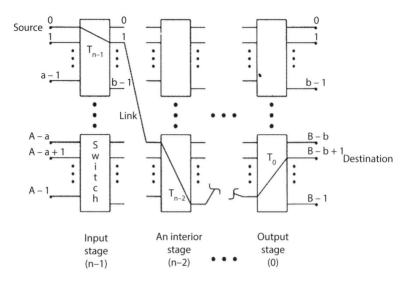

Figure 7.5 A Generic MIN Diagram Detailing One Path.

Figure 7.5 shows MIN hardware in the most general terms; dots indicate items that may repeat. MINs are composed of a collection of *switches* and *links* between switches. A signal may enter or leave a network through a *port*. A network with A input ports and B output ports is an A × B network.

A switch may be viewed as a very simple network. Switches are multiport devices; the number of ports and the port-to-port connections supported within a switch vary among switch designs. A *crossbar* switch can simultaneously connect, in any pattern, a number of input/output port pairs equal to the minimum of the number of inputs and the number of outputs. A *selector* switch connects only one of its inputs to one of its outputs at a time.

The term *network component* may denote any element of the structure of a network. An interconnection network may consist of a single *stage*, or bank of switches and may require that data pass through the network more than once to reach its destination. A MIN is constructed from two or more stages of switches, and typically is designed so that data can be sent to the desired destination by one pass through the network.

MINs can be considered from either a topological (graphical) or algebraic viewpoint. The *topology* of a network is the pattern of connections in its structure, where the pattern can be represented by a graph. Topology is determined by switch design and the pattern of links. Different MINs are often compared graphically because comparison by topology is independent of hardware. When one network is said to be an instance of another, it is the network graphs being compared. Nodes in the graph of a MIN can be numbered, and then a MIN can be described in terms of the algebraic relations among the nodes. The algebraic model is useful in discussing control and communication routing strategy.

There are three basic forms of connection through a network. A *one-to-one connection* passes information from one network port, the *source*, to another network port, the *destination*. The exact route taken by the information is its *path*. Multiple one-to-one connections may be active simultaneously. A *permutation connection* is a set of one-to-one connections such that no two one-to-one connections have the same source or destination. Such connections are meaningful only in the context of networks with equal number of sources and destinations. Information flow from one source simultaneously to two or more destinations is supported by a *broadcast connection*, and the route taken is a *broadcast path*.

Routing tags are a way of describing a path through a network and providing for distributed network control. For MINs, tags often take the form of a multidigit integer, each successive digit encoding the setting for the switch in the next stage along a desired path. Control is distributed if devices using the network generate their own routing tags and network switches can set themselves based on tag information. Figure 7.5 shows a switch in stages n −1, n − 2, and 0 being set, respectively, by tag digits T_{n-1}, T_{n-2}, and T_0. Routing tags are particularly important for fault-tolerant MINs since they should be able to specify a functioning path if one exists; tag limitations translate into fault-tolerance limitations.

There are three methods for sources to generate routing tags that specify a fault-free path. With *nonadaptive routing* a source learns of a fault only when the path it is attempting to establish reaches the faulty network component. Notice of the fault is sent to the source, which tries the next alternative path. This approach requires little hardware, but may have poor performance. There are two forms of *adaptive routing*. With *notification on demand* a source maintains a table of faults it has encountered in attempting to establish paths and uses this information to guide future routing. With *broadcast notification* of a fault, all sources are notified of faulty components as they are diagnosed.

A fault-free path need not be specified by a source if routing tags can be modified in response to faults encountered as a path is followed or established. This *dynamic routing* can be accomplished in MINs constructed of switches capable of performing the necessary routing tag revisions.

The following section explores the network topologies in Multistage Interconnection Networks (MINs). Various inherent properties include path establishment, distributed routing tag control, and partitionability are presented. In general, the multistage networks have analogous, but not identical, properties. The standard networks and the hardware modifications made to provide redundancy, from less to more extensive, are introduced. Many possible techniques exist, including adding an extra stage of switches, varying switch size, adding extra links, and adding extra ports. Finally, some irregular MINs that have different connection patterns between stages are also discussed.

7.1.5   Fault-Tolerant

A *fault-tolerant* MIN is one that provides service, in at least some cases, even when it contains a faulty component or components. A fault can be either permanent or transient, unless stated otherwise, it is assumed that faults are permanent. Fault tolerance is defined only with respect to a chosen *fault-tolerance model*, which has two parts. The *fault model* characterizes all faults assumed to occur, stating the failure modes (if any) for each network component. The *fault-tolerance criterion* is the condition that must be met for the network to be said to have tolerated a given fault or faults.

Fault models may or may not correspond closely to predicted or actual experience with MIN hardware. In particular, a fault model may be chosen with characteristics that simplify reliability analysis, even if those characteristics depart widely from reality (such as assuming certain network components never fail). While fault-tolerance criteria typically closely reflect the normal (fault-free) operational capability of a network, this need not be so. The variability of fault-tolerance models hinders comparison of the engineering characteristics of fault-tolerant MINs.

A network is *single-fault tolerant* if it can function as specified by its fault-tolerance criterion despite any single fault conforming to its fault model. More generally, if any set of i faults can be tolerated, then a network is *i-fault tolerant*. A network that can tolerate some instances of i faults is robust although not i-fault tolerant.

Many fault-tolerant systems require fault diagnosis (detection and location) to achieve their fault tolerance. Techniques such as test patterns, dynamic parity checking, and write/read-back/verify is used in various MINs. Techniques for fault-tolerant design can be categorized by whether they involve modifying the topology (graph) of the system. Three well-known methods that do not modify topology are error-correcting codes, bit-slice implementation with spare bit slices, and duplicating an entire network (this changes the topology of the larger system using the network). These approaches to fault tolerance can be applied to MINs. A number of techniques have also been developed tailored closely to the nature of MINs and their use.

7.2   Multistage Cube Network

Figure 7.6 shows the *generalized cube* network topology for N inputs and N outputs. The generalized cube topology was introduced as a standard for comparing different types of multistage cube networks. It has n = $\log_2$ N stages, numbered from 0 to n − 1, where each stage consists of a set of N lines (links), numbered from 0 to N − 1, connected to N/2 interchange boxes. Each interchange box is a two-input, two-output device that can be set as shown in Figure 7.6. The labels of the links entering the upper and lower inputs of an interchange box are used as the labels for the upper and lower outputs, respectively. At stage i, links whose numbers differ only in the i-th bit position are paired at interchange boxes. PE j is attached to network input j and output j.

The name *multistage cube network* will be used to refer to the network consisting of the generalized cube topology and interchange boxes with the capabilities shown in Figure 7.6, where each interchange box is controlled independently. The term multistage cube has its origin in the multidimensional cube network. In a multidimensional cube network, the vertices can be labeled in binary so those vertices whose labels differ only in bit position i are connected across dimension i. This pairing of vertices that differ in bit

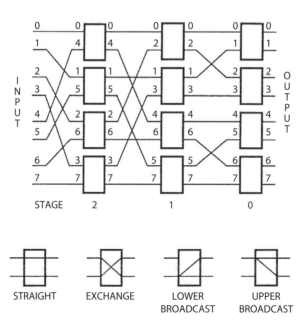

Figure 7.6 Multistage Cube Network for N = 8.

position i along dimension i corresponds to pairing links whose labels differ only in bit position i at an interchange box in stage i of the multistage cube network.

One-to-one connections use the straight and exchange interchange box settings. To go from a source $S = s_{n-1}...s_1 s_0$ to a destination $D = d_{n-1}...d_1 d_0$, where $0 \le s_i, d_i \le k -1$, for $0 \le i \le n - 1$, the stage i interchange box in the path from S to D should be set as follows: if $d_i = s_i$, then the interchange box is set to straight, and if $d_i = \bar{s}_i$ (a lower input connecting to an upper output or an upper input connecting to a lower output), then the interchange box is set to exchange. For example, if $s_2 s_1 s_0 = 110$ and $d_2 d_1 d_0 = 000$, then the interchange boxes are set as shown in Figure 7.7. The links that a message from S to D uses is $s_{n-1}...s_1 s_0$ before stage n – 1, $d_{n-1} s_{n-2}...s_1 s_0$ after stage n – 1, $d_{n-1} d_{n-2} s_{n-3}...s_1 s_0$ after stage n – 2, ..., and $d_{n-1}...d_1 d_0$ after stage 0. In general, the link that a message from S to D uses after stage i is $d_{n-1}...d_{i+1} d_i s_{i-1}...s_1 s_0$. For the example in Figure 7.7, the links traversed are $s_2 s_1 s_0 = 110$ at the input, $d_2 s_1 s_0 = 010$ after stage 2, $d_2 d_1 s_0 = 000$ after stage 1, and $d_2 d_1 d_0 = 000$ after stage 0. Because the stage i output link used in the path from S to D must be $d_{n-1}...d_{i+1} d_i s_{i-1}...s_1 s_0$, there is only one path from a given source to a given destination.

This unique path property limits the fault tolerance of the generalized cube topology in that a single network fault will prevent some source/destination pairs from being able to communicate. A conflict occurs in a multistage cube network when the messages on the two input links of an interchange box want to go out the same output link. Typically, when a situation like this arises, one message is blocked and must wait until the other has completed its transmission. Both requests cannot be accommodated simultaneously.

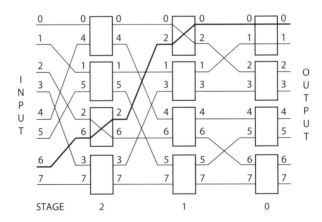

Figure 7.7 The Path from Input 6 to Output 0 for N = 8.

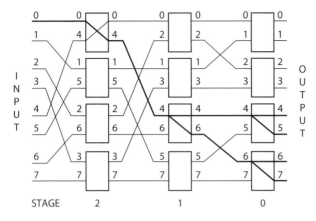

Figure 7.8 The Broadcast Path from Input 0 to Outputs 4, 5, 6, and 7 for N = 8.

A *broadcast* (one-to-many) *connection* is performed when the lower and/or upper broadcast states of interchange boxes are used in a path. For example, in Figure 7.8 input 0 broadcasts to outputs 4, 5, 6, and 7.

Network control for the multistage cube is distributed among the PEs by using a routing tag as the header (first item) of each message to be transmitted through the network. For one-to-one (nonbroadcast) connections, an n-bit routing tag can be computed by the source PE from its number $S = s_{n-1}...s_1 s_0$ and desired destination PE number $D = d_{n-1}...d_1 d_0$. The routing tag $T = t_{n-1}...t_1 t_0 = S \oplus D$ (where $\oplus$ means bitwise exclusive-OR) is called the XOR (exclusive-OR) routing tag. When an interchange box in the network at stage i receives a message, it examines bit t_i of the tag. If $t_i = 0$, the straight connection is used, because $t_i = 0$ implies $d_i = s_i$. If $t_i = 1$, an exchange is performed, because $t_i = 1$ implies $d_i = \overline{s_i}$. If N = 8, S = 6 = 110, and D = 0 = 000, then the routing tag T = 110, and the corresponding interchange box settings from input to output are exchange ($t_2 = 1$), exchange ($t_1 = 1$), and straight ($t_0 = 0$), as shown in Figure 7.7.

The same tag used to route data from S to D can be used to route data from D to S because the exclusive-OR operation is commutative (i.e., $S \oplus D = D \oplus S$). This can be used to confirm receipt of the data. Because each network destination D knows its own address (output port number), the source address S (input port number) can be computed from the tag: $S = T \oplus D$.

Another approach to routing tags is the destination tag scheme, where the destination $D = d_{n-1}...d_1 d_0$ is the tag sent as the header. The upper output link of a stage i interchange box always has a 0 in the i-th bit position of its label, while the lower output link always has a 1. Therefore, taking the upper output link leads to a destination where $d_i = 0$, while taking the lower output link leads to a destination where $d_i = 1$. Therefore, when an interchange box in the network at stage i receives a message, it examines d_i: if $d_i = 0$ the upper output is taken, if $d_i = 1$ the lower output is taken. For the example, from source 6 to destination 0 in Figure 7.7, the upper output of the stage 2 interchange box is taken ($d_2 = 0$), the upper output of the stage 1 interchange box is taken ($d_1 = 0$), and the upper output of the stage 0 interchange box is taken (($d_0 = 0$). This same destination tag ($D = 000$) can be used to route data from any input to output 0.

The advantages of the destination scheme over the XOR method are easier to compare the destination tag that arrives against its own destination address and determine if the message arrived at the correct network output (if it did not, the network must be faulty). The destination tag scheme has the disadvantage that it cannot be used to determine the source, as the XOR scheme can. By sending the source address along with the destination tag or sending the destination address along with the XOR tag, both methods can have the capability both to determine if the data arrived at the proper destination and to identify its source. The destination tag scheme is more practical, while the XOR scheme is more mathematically pleasing. A broadcast routing tag scheme that consists of an n-bit broadcast mask along with either type of n-bit routing tag can be used to specify a variety of broadcast connections.

The partitionability of the multistage cube network is the ability to divide the network into independent subnetworks of different sizes so that each subnetwork of size $N' \leq N$ has all the interconnection capabilities of a multistage cube network built to be of size N'. The methods for partitioning the multistage cube network assume a PE-to-PE configuration, where PE i is connected to both network input i and output i, so both input i and output i must belong to the same partition. These methods can also be used to partition the processor-to-memory configuration, but there are some partitioning that will support the processor-to-memory configuration and not the PE-to-PE.

7.3   Extra-Stage Cube Network

The extra-stage cube (ESC) network is formed from the generalized cube by adding an extra stage to the input side of the network along with multiplexers and demultiplexers at the input and output stages, respectively. In addition, dual I/O links to and from the devices using the network are required. Stage n is connected like stage 0; that is, links that differ in the low-order bit are paired. Figure 7.9 illustrates the ESC for $N = 8$.

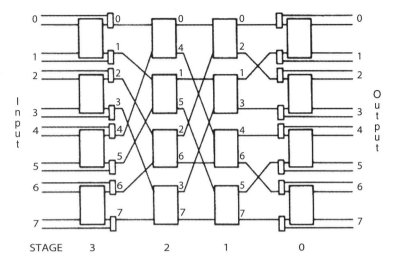

Figure 7.9 The Extra-Stage Cube Network for N = 8.

Stage n and stage 0 can each be enabled or disabled (bypassed). A stage is enabled when its switches are being used to provide interconnection; it is disabled when its switches are being bypassed. Enabling and disabling of stage n or 0 are demonstrated by Figure 7.10. Having multiple ports per device using the ESC is equivalent to the input demultiplexer and output multiplexer arrangement originally described for the network.

Normally, the network will be set so that stage n is disabled and stage 0 is enabled. The resulting structure matches that of the generalized cube. If a fault is found after running fault detection and location tests, the network is reconfigured. A fault in a stage n switch requires no change in network configuration; stage n remains disabled. If the fault occurs in stage 0, then stage n is enabled and stage 0 is disabled; i.e., stage n replaces the function of stage 0. For a fault in a link or in a switch in stages n − 1 to 1, both stages n and 0 will be enabled.

Enabling both stages n and 0 provides two distinct paths between any source and destination, at least one of which must be fault-free given any single fault in the network. ESC multiple-fault tolerance is enhanced by individually enabling and disabling stage n and 0 switches.

The ESC fault model assumes that [4]:

1. any network component can fail,
2. faulty components are unusable, and
3. faults occur independently.

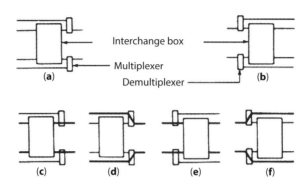

Figure 7.10 Detail of Input Stage Switch with Multiplexer for Enabling and Disabling (a), Output Stage Switch with Demultiplexer for Enabling and Disabling (b), Input Stage Switch Enabled (c), Input Stage Switch Disabled (d), Output Stage Switch Enabled (e), Output Stage Switch Disabled (f).

The ESC fault-tolerance criterion is retention of the fault-free interconnection capability of a generalized cube MIN for one-to-one and broadcast connections. This corresponds to full access, the ability to connect any MIN input to any output. The ESC is single fault tolerant and robust in the presence of multiple faults. The ESC can be controlled by a simple extension of the routing tags used for the generalized cube. The tags are readily computed as the bitwise exclusive-OR of the number of the network input and output ports to be connected, perhaps modified by information as to the location of a possible fault.

7.4 Shuffle-Exchange Network

The shuffle-exchange multistage interconnection network (SEN) is one network in a large class of topologically equivalent MINs that include the omega, indirect binary n-cube, baseline, and generalized cube. Figure 7.11 is an example of an 8×8 SEN. Each switching element (SE), the basic building block of a SEN, can be viewed as a 2×2 SEN. The SE can either transmit the inputs straight or has crossed connections.

A SEN has $N = 2^n$ inputs, termed sources (S), and 2^n outputs termed destinations (D). There is a unique path between each source-destination pair. The SEN has n stages and each stage has $N/2$ switching elements. The network complexity, defined as the total number of switching elements in the MIN, is $(N/2) (\log_2 N)$ which for the 8×8 SEN is 12 SE's. The position of switching element i in stage j is represented by $SE_{i,j}$.

The SEN is a self-routing network. That is, a message from any source to a given destination is routed through the network according to the binary

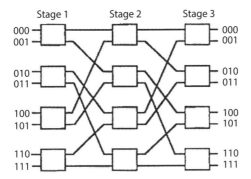

Figure 7.11 8 x 8 Shuffle-Exchange Multistage Interconnection Network.

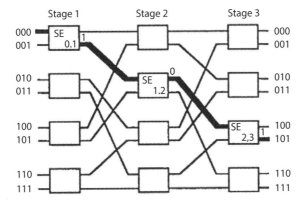

Figure 7.12 Routing for Communication Between S = 000 and D = 101.

representation of the destination's address. For example, from S = 000 sends a message to D = 101, the routing can be described as follows: S = 000 presents the address of D = 101 plus the message for D to the SE in stage 1 to which S = 000 ($SE_{0,1}$) is connected. The first bit of the destination address (1) is used by $SE_{0,1}$ for routing. So output link 1 of $SE_{0,1}$ is used. At $SE_{1,2}$ the second bit of D (0) is used and output link 0 of $SE_{1,2}$ is chosen. Finally, at $SE_{2,3}$ the third bit of D (1) is used and output link 1 of $SE_{2,3}$ is selected. Figure 7.12 shows this S-D connection.

7.5   Shuffle-Exchange Network with an Additional Stage

An N × N SEN+ network is an N × N SEN with an additional stage. Figure 7.13 shows an 8 × 8 SEN+ [5]. The first stage (labeled stage 0) is

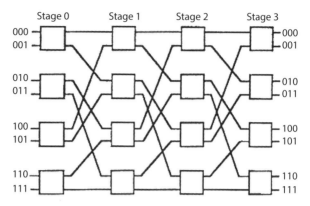

Figure 7.13 8 x 8 SEN with an Extra Stage.

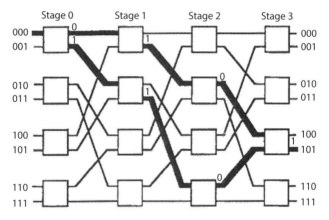

Figure 7.14 Two Paths for Routing Communication Between S = 000 and D = 101 in the 8 x 8 SEN+.

the additional stage and will require implementation of a different control strategy. While several control strategies for the SEN+ network can be selected, the strategy chosen may affect both the bandwidth and the reliability of the network.

The reason for adding a stage to the SEN is to allow two paths for communication between each S and any D. While the paths in the first and last stages of the SEN+ are not disjoint, the paths in the intermediate stages do traverse disjoint links. As can be seen in Figure 7.14, S = 000 can reach D = 101 by two paths. In this case, the path redundancy is achieved in the SEN+ at the expense of one extra stage added to the SEN.

The control strategy allows a switching element in stage 0 to use the T (straight) setting until a failure in a SE along the path from a given S to a given

D is detected. At that time, the SE in stage 0 is placed in the X (exchange) setting for all future accesses between that S-D pair. In this way, it is shown that two paths between each S-D pair given that the failures occur only in the intermediate stages of the SEN+. It is recognized that in actual implementations, the network should be reconfigured to reduce congestion.

Figure 7.13 shows that the switch complexity (the total number of switching elements in the network) for the 8 x 8 SEN+ is 16. In general, the switch complexity for the N x N SEN+ is N/2 ($\log_2$ N + 1). Thus, the additional cost of the SEN+ is N/2 switches or a fractional increase of 1/$\log_2$ N, is small for a large N. In the next chapter, how much the increase in the redundancy improves the reliability of the SEN will be evaluated.

7.6   Gamma Network

The Gamma network is an interconnection network connecting N = 2^n inputs to N outputs [6]. It consists of ($\log_2$ N) + 1 stages with N switches per stage. In all but the first and last stages, each switching element is a 3 input, 3 output switch. The first, or input stage, consists of 1 input, 3 output switches, and the last stage consists of 3 input, 1 output switches. The stages are linked in such a way that redundant paths exist between the input and output terminals.

A message from a source can change its route at n points before reaching its destination. There are three possible interconnections at stage i to stage i + 1: the data from cell (switching element) j at stage i [$0 \leq j \leq N - 1$ and $0 \leq i \leq (\log_2$ N)] can take the straight path to output cell j, or take the upward path to reach cell $(j - 2^i)$ mod N, or take the downward path to reach cell $(j + 2^i)$ mod N. The expression x mod y is the remainder of x divided by y (i.e., $(7 + 2^1)$ mod 8 is 1). With each message, a routing tag is used to guide the message through the network. If the source number is x and the destination number is y, where x and y lie in the range 0 and N – 1, then $\delta = y - x$ will be the tag value. It is interesting to observe that except for tag value 0, there are always multiple representations for routing tags. This means, for a source-x and destination-y pair, there is only one path if x = y, and more than one path if x ≠ y.

Each digit in the routing tag will be either 1, 0, or -1. The digits are numbered such that the first digit is most significant, and the nth digit is least significant. Now consider gamma network of Figure 7.15, the flow of data from source 2 to destination 5 when N = 8. The difference between x and y is 3, which in binary form is 011. The binary redundant forms for the value 3 are (0)(1)(1), (1)(0)(-1), and (1)(-1)(1). The difference between

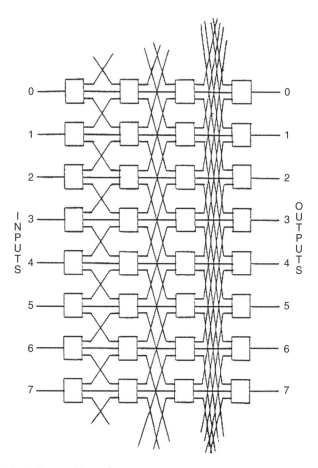

Figure 7.15 8 x 8 Gamma Network.

2 and 5 modulo N can also be viewed as $3 - N = -5$, which can be represented either as $(-1)(0)(-1)$ or $(-1)(-1)(1)$. All redundant representations for the values 3 and -5 will be valid tags for routing data from source 2 to destination 5.

In this network, at any switching element three different messages can arrive at the same time. At the ith stage, a cell j can receive inputs from j, $(j - 2^{i+1})$ mod N, $(j + 2^{i+1})$ mod N. These three messages will respectively have 0, 1, and (-1) in the ith digit of their tags. The three messages can be routed to three different cells if the ith digits of their tags are all different. However, if any two of them have the same i^{th} digit in their tags then there is a conflict. Such conflicts can be avoided in most cases by using alternate forms for the tags, except when tag value is 0. Therefore, there is considerable flexibility in selecting routes for permuting data in this network.

7.7   Extra-Stage Gamma Network

The Gamma network is based on the Plus-Minus-2^i connection patterns. In such a network there exist multiple paths to connect a source S to a destination D, except when S = D. The number of paths for (S, D) is a function of the tag value (D - S) modulo N, and the size of the network N [7].

The extra-stage gamma network is constructed by adding an extra stage to the original gamma network. Multiple paths are provided for all the tag values including 0. The extra stage can be any stage out of n = $\log_2$ N stages of the original network. The extra stage of 0, 1, -1 connection patterns gives the most uniform distribution, and also results in a 1-fault tolerant interconnection network.

Figure 7.16 shows that there are 9 possible paths for S = 3 and D = 3 connection pair. This is one of the advantages of the extra-stage gamma

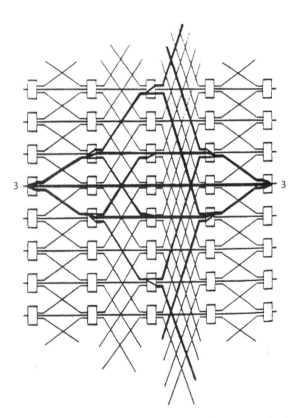

Figure 7.16 8 x 8 Extra-Stage Gamma Network with 9 Paths Between (3,3) Pair Connection.

network comparing with the original gamma network, that has only a single path when S = D. Thus, the additional stage provides more redundant paths and higher network reliability.

7.8 Dynamic Redundancy Network

The dynamic redundancy (DR) network has N + Spare I/O ports and $\log_2$ N stages, each with N + Spare switches followed by 3(N + Spare) links. There are N + Spare output switches. Each switch j at stage i of the network has three links to stage i −1. One is connected to switch $(j - 2^i)$ mod (N + Spare), the second to switch j, and the third to switch $(j + 2^i)$ mod (N + Spare). The DR output switches are its output ports. Figure 7.17 shows a DR network for N = 8 and Spare = 2 [8]. The spare I/O ports allow

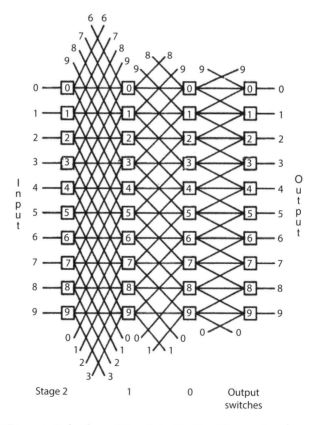

Figure 7.17 Dynamic Redundancy Network for N = 8 and Spare = 2.

spares of the devices using the network, thus providing fault tolerance for devices.

A row of a DR network contains all the switches having the same address, all links incident out of them, and the associated network input and output links. A row has the same address as its switches. Two rows of the DR network are said to be adjacent if their addresses are consecutive (mod N + Spare).

The DR fault model is the same as for the extra-stage cube (ESC): any component may fail. Its fault tolerance criterion is retention of the ability to perform any set of simultaneous connections possible with the generalized cube. This is a stricter criterion than used for the ESC.

When there are no faults, rows 0 to N −1 are used to emulate the generalized cube network. If a component of row j is found to be faulty, the network is reconfigured so that the switches physically numbered p are logically renumbered t(p), where t(p) = (p − j − S) mod (N + Spare). As long as N adjacent rows remain, the DR network can contain the generalized cube subgraph and thus act as a fault-tolerant generalized cube.

7.9   Improved Enhanced Augmented Data Manipulator Network

Data Manipulator (DM) networks is a member of the Plus-Minus-2^i (PM2I) connection patterns. The network structure and its properties are identical with the Gamma network. However, it does not have any fault tolerant capability because identical switches in different stages are set by the same control. To overcome this limitation, the Augmented Data Manipulator was proposed [9]. Each switch in this network can be set independently of others that make the ADM network a two paths network. The problem is when the two paths leading to the same destination share straight link(s) and therefore there is no alternative path to route data through it. This condition makes the ADM network not a true fault-tolerant network.

To achieve the fault tolerance capability of the ADM network, the Enhanced Augmented Data Manipulator (EADM) network was proposed. The fault tolerance capability is achieved by adding extra links to the original data manipulator. Two extra links (called half-links) are added to each switch in stages 1 to n − 1. Half-links connect switch m in stage i to switches $(m + 2^{i-1})$ mod N and $(m − 2^{i-1})$ mod N in stage i + 1. The EADM is considered as single-fault MIN assuming that the input and the output stages are fault free.

The improved EADM (IEADM) network has the basic topology of the original EADM network. To improve the fault tolerance capabilities of the network, the following changes are proposed in the basic EADM network [10]:

1. Multiplexers in the output stage of the original EADM are replaced by ordinary switches. Thus, the number of stages in an N x N IEADM network ($N = 2^m$) is m + 1.
2. Inputs are connected to the first stage in the network (stage 0) using the three functions (f_{-1}, f_0, f_{+1}), i.e. each input is connected to three switches according to the three functions.
3. Outputs are connected to stage m using the same three functions and the half-link functions. It should be noted that each output will be connected to exactly two switches. Figure 7.18 shows a 4 x 4 IEADM network.

The fault-model to be used for the IEADM network is the strictest fault-model. The assumptions under this model are:

1. Any component of the network can fail regardless of its location in the network. Switches or links in stages 0, 1,..., m can fail.
2. Faulty components are totally unusable.
3. Faults occur independently.

7.10   Improved Logical Neighborhood Network

The Logical Neighborhood (LN) network is derived from the data manipulator and the cube networks. The fault-tolerance capability is achieved by

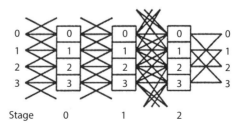

Figure 7.18 4 x 4 IEADM Network.

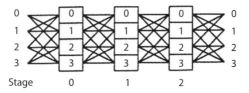

Figure 7.19 4 x 4 ILN Network.

creating redundant paths using extra links and a new routing algorithm. It is considered as an (m − 1)-fault tolerant MIN assuming that the input and the output stages are fault free, where m is the number of stages in the network.

The improved LN (ILN) network is an improved version of the LN network [11]. It has the same basic topology as the original LN network and the same idea, applied to enhance the fault tolerance capability of the IEADM network, is applied here. In this case, each input is connected to all switches in stage 0 whose binary addresses differ in at most one bit from its binary address. Each output is connected to all switches in stage m whose binary addresses differ in at most one bit from its binary address. Figure 7.19 shows a 4 x 4 ILN network. The ILN network uses the same fault-model and the same routing algorithm used in the IEADM network.

7.11   Comparison

Table 7.1 summarizes the network fault tolerance information presented in this chapter [12]. It lists: the possible faults that can occur in each network under the assumed fault model; whether or not faulty components are usable; the fault-tolerance criterion; the method by which the network copes with faults; whether the network is single-fault tolerant; and how the network performs with multiple faults. The phrase "interior switch only" used in the table is another way of saying input and output switches are assumed fault-free.

Table 7.2 summarizes structural characteristics of the networks [12]. Switch type, number of stages of switches, number of switches per stage, and number of links between stages of switches are four parameters relevant to both implementation cost and achievable fault tolerance. Networks with high switch and link counts may require high package counts and hence cost more to produce than less complex structures. Networks with high package counts are more likely to experience failure during a given period of time. The nature of real failures must be taken into account, along with expected reliability, package count, network topology and operation

Table 7.1 Summary of Fault Tolerance Information for the Observed Networks.

Network	Fault Model	Fault-Tolerance Criterion	Fault-Tolerance Method	Single-Fault Tolerant	Multiple-Fault Tolerant
Multistage cube	Any component; unusable	Full access	Single route only	No	No
Extra-stage cube	Any component; unusable	Full access	Alternative route	Yes	Robust
Shuffle-exchange	Interior switch only; unusable	Full access	Single route only	No	No
Extra-stage shuffle	Interior switch only; unusable	Full access	Alternative route	Yes	Robust
Gamma	Interior switch or link; unusable	Full access	Possible alternative route	No	No
Extra-stage Gamma	Interior switch or link; unusable	Full access	Possible alternative route	Yes	Robust
Dynamic redundancy	Any component; unusable	Full access	Alternative (spare)	Yes	Limited robustness
IEADM	Interior switch or link; unusable	Full access	Alternative routes	Yes	Two-fault tolerant
ILN	Interior switch or link; unusable	Full access	Alternative routes	Yes	Two-fault tolerant

Table 7.2 Summary of Structural Characteristics of the Observed Networks.

Network	Network Ports per Source or Destination	Switch Type	Number of Stages	Number of Switches per Stage	Number of Links per Stage
Multistage cube	2	Four-state interchange box	$\log_2 N$	N/2	N
Extra-stage cube	2	Four-state interchange box	$1 + \log_2 N$	N/2	N
Shuffle-exchange	2	Four-state interchange box	$\log_2 N$	N/2	N
Extra-stage shuffle	2	Four-state interchange box	$1 + \log_2 N$	N/2	N
Gamma	1	3×3 crossbar	$1 + \log_2 N$	N	3N
Extra-stage Gamma	1	3×3 crossbar	$2 + \log_2 N$	N	3N
Dynamic redundancy	1	3×3 mux/demux	$\log_2 N$	N + S	$3 \star (N + S)$
IEADM	1	5×5 crossbar	$1 + \log_2 N$	N	5N interior, 3N input stage, 2N output stage
ILN	1	3×3 crossbar	$1 + \log_2 N$	N	3N

protocol to estimate a cost/fault-tolerance performance ratio for a particular network.

Despite the growing research on fault-tolerant MINs, the results often have limitations, including unreasonably optimistic fault-tolerance models, and increased data routing complexity. To place the observed networks in perspective, a hypothetical fault-tolerant MIN should have the following ideal engineering characteristics:

1. Fault model – any network component can fail, and failed components are unusable.
2. Fault-tolerance criterion – full access.
3. Routing complexity – as low as any observed network.
4. Hardware complexity – as low as any observed network.
5. Fault-tolerance capability – singe-fault tolerant and robust with respect to multiple faults.

Finally, some techniques that alter the topology of a MIN for better fault tolerance are concluded below:

1. Adding an extra stage (ESC, SEN+, extra-stage gamma)
2. Increasing the number of network ports slightly (dynamic redundancy)
3. Completing inherent partial redundancy in a MIN (IEADM, ILN)
4. Adding extra links
5. Varying switch size and number of stages
6. Increasing switch size and adding corresponding links
7. Replicating a MIN and stages of switches
8. Replicating a MIN and adding an extra stage
9. Combination of these techniques

References

1. Duato, J., Yalmanchili, S., and Ni, L. M., *Interconnection Networks an Engineering Approach*, IEEE Computer Society, Los Alamitos, CA, 1997.
2. Ni, L. M., Gui, Y., and Moore, S., Performance Evaluation of Switch-Based Wormhole Networks, *Proceeding of the 1995 International Conference on Parallel Processing*, vol. 1, 32–40, August 1995.
3. Hwang, K. and Briggs, F. A., *Computer Architecture and Parallel Processing*, McGraw-Hill, New York, 1984.

4. Adams III, G. B. and Siegel, H. J., The Extra Stage Cube: A Fault Tolerant Interconnection Network for Supersystems, *IEEE Transactions on Computers*, 443–454, May 1982.

5. Blake, J. and Trivedi, K. S., Reliabilities of Two Fault-Tolerant Interconnection Networks, *Proceeding of the Eighteenth International Symposium on Fault Tolerant Computing*, 300–305, June 1988.

6. Parker, D. S. and Raghavendra, C. S., The Gamma Network, *IEEE Transactions on Computers*, vol. C-33 (4), 367–373, April 1984.

7. Lee, K. Y. and Hegazy, W., The Extra Stage Gamma Network, *Computer*, 175–182, 1986.

8. Siegel, H. J., *Interconnection Networks for Large Scale Parallel Processing: Theory and Case Studies*, Lexington Books, Lexington, MA, 1985.

9. McMillen, R. J. and Siegel, H. J., Routing Schemes for the Augmented Data Manipulator Network in an MIMD System, *IEEE Transactions on Computers*, vol. C-31 (12), 184–196, December 1982.

10. Abd-El-Barr, M. and Abed, O., Fault-Tolerance and Terminal Reliability for a Class of Data Manipulator Networks, *Computer*, 225–229, 1995.

11. Smith, S. D., Siegel, H. J., McMillen, R. J., and Adams, G. B., Use of the Augmented Data Manipulator Multistage Network for SIMD Machines, *Proceedings of the International Conference on Parallel Processing*, 75–78, 1980.

12. Adams III, G. B., Agrawal, D. P., and Siegel, H. J., A Survey and Comparison of Fault-Tolerant Multistage Interconnection Networks, *IEEE Transactions on Computers*, vol. 20, no. 6, 14–27, June 1987.

8

Network Reliability Evaluation Methods

8.1 Overview of Network Reliability

The problem of determining the reliability of a complex system, whose components are subject to failure, has received considerable attention in the statistical, engineering, and operations research literature. Indeed, in certain situations, improving the reliability of a system can be more consequential than reducing its cost. Reliability analysis can be applied to a variety of practical systems, ranging from large-scale telecommunication, transportation, and mechanical systems, to the microelectronic scale of integrated circuits. In addition, the reliability of computer software, as well as computer hardware, has become increasingly important in commercial and military applications. In example such as these, two broad objectives are addressed by reliability theory: assessing the reliability of a given system (analysis) and designing as reliable a system as possible from the given components (synthesis) [1].

Network reliability is commonly arises from the interconnection of various elements in the form of a network or a graph. For example, the nodes of a multistage interconnection network might represent the physical locations of switching elements and its edges might represent existing communication links between switching elements. In realistic settings, the elements of a network, its nodes or edges or both, are subject to failure, but in most analysis only the links are considered as failing components. At any stage, each element is either working or failed, as a result, the network itself is also either working or failed. In the multistage interconnection networks example, working might mean that a distinguished input switching element and distinguished output switching element are able to communicate over operational links of the network, while failure means that there is no complete transmission path in the system.

8.2   Network Model

A network G = (N, E) consists of a set N of nodes together with a set E of edges, representing pairs of nodes. If the pairs are ordered, it is called a directed network and (i, j) represents the directed edge joining node i to node j. If the pairs are considered to be unordered, then it is called an undirected network and the edge joining i and j is represented by [i, j]. In either case the edge between i and j is said to be incident to both i and j; in this case nodes i and j are said to be adjacent. For most purposes, an undirected network can be adequately represented as a directed network by associating oppositely directed edges (i, j) and (j, i) with each undirected edge [i, j].

At any instant the elements of the network (nodes and/or edges) will be in either of two possible states, working or failed. In deterministic networks it is considered that working elements can be successfully attacked by an adversary, resulting in their failure or inactivation. The failure of an edge means that it is removed from the network, while the failure of a node means that the node and all its incident edges are removed from the network. In deterministic network models, the focus is typically on evaluating the worst-case performance of the network. In this case, the adversary intelligently chooses certain elements to inactivate, resulting in the maximum damage to the network.

By contrast, in probabilistic networks it is usually assumed that at any instant, elements fail randomly and independently of one another, according to certain known probabilities. Specifically each node i has an associated reliability p_i indicating the probability that it is operational, and each edge k has a reliability p_k, the probability that it is operational. Thus at any instant, the elements of the network fail independently with probabilities $q_i = 1 - p_i$ and $q_k = 1 - p_k$, respectively. In these circumstances, one would be interested in assessing the average performance of the network, under the assumption of random failures. It is also possible to allow for dependent failure modes, at the expense of added data-gathering requirements and increased subsequent computation. For example, the edges incident with a given node might be subject to certain common influences, and these edges might therefore tend to fail together, rather than independently; or the failure of one edge might place additional stress on the other operating incident edges, making them more likely to fail.

8.3   Network Operations

Reliability of the network is concerned with the ability of a network to carry out its desired network operation successfully. In our case, interconnection networks for processor-processor and processor-memory information exchanges in multiprocessing parallel processing systems, contribute appreciably to the performance as well as the reliability of the overall system. The reliability measures of particular interest are: terminal reliability (TR), broadcast reliability (BR), and network reliability (NR).

1. *Terminal Reliability* (TR). Terminal reliability, generally used as a measure of robustness of a MIN, is the probability of existence of at least one fault free path between a designated pair of input (s) and output (t) terminals (two terminal). This is denoted by R_{st} (G), where G is the network representing the system. G can be directed or undirected. If G is directed, there should at least be one directed path between s and t.

2. *Broadcast Reliability* (BR). Another useful measure of the reliability of a MIN is its ability to broadcast data from a given input terminal to all the output terminals of the network. A network is said to have failed when a connection cannot be made from the given input terminal to at least one of the output terminals.

3. *Network Reliability* (NR). The network reliability is defined as the probability that there exists a connection between each input to all outputs (all terminal).

8.4   Approaches for Calculating Network Reliability

This section provides several general approaches for calculating the reliability of probabilistic networks. It is supposed that G = (N, E) is a directed

network, having a distinguished source node s and distinguished destination node t. The nodes of G are assumed to be perfect, whereas the edges
$k \in E$ are assumed to fail in a statistically independent fashion with known
probabilities $q_k = 1 - p_k$. Of particular concern here will be the terminal
reliability measure R_{st} (G), the probability that there is a path of operative
edges from s to t in G.

8.4.1   Minpaths Method

The network reliability can be analyzed by using a probabilistic graph. The
graph whose edges randomly fail and is represented by G = (N, E), where
N is the set of nodes, and E is the set of edges. The number of nodes and
edges are denoted as $|N| = n$ and $|E| = m$ respectively. Each edge i, j in E is
operational with probability P_{ij}.

   The s-t minpaths is a minimal set of links that functioning ensures
that source node s and destination node t can communicate with each
other. Operational network is defined as the possibility of connecting
between the s and t with at least one chain of its links. The set of links is
called a path. In general, there are several possible such paths in the network. Each path represents a series connection of corresponding links.
The path E_k^* is defined as a subset of network units, such that if all units
of E_k^* are operational, the network poles are connected although all other
remaining units fail. These remaining units may fail without any influ-
ence on the network's connectivity. Therefore, it is possible to delete them
without changing the network connectivity. This connection brought the
idea of a simple path. A simple path E_k is the minimal set of units x_j,
where $x_j \in E_k$ and when at least one unit of a path fails, the path will be
disconnected.

Denote the structure function of path E_k by

$$a_k = \bigcap_{j \in E_k} x_j$$

A network with only one path is a series system. If all of the possible N
paths in a terminal network are considered, the structure function can be
represented as

$$\delta(X) = \bigcup_{1 \le k \le N} a_k(x)$$

Therefore the network can be presented as a parallel connection of all different paths.

An example of such a representation of a bridge network is depicted in
Figure 8.1.

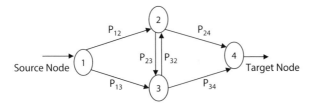

Figure 8.1 A Simple Probability Graph.

The s-t minpaths when s = 1 and t = 4 are:
$P_1 = \{(1,2), (2,4)\}$,
$P_2 = \{(1,3), (3,4)\}$,
$P_3 = \{(1,2), (2,3), (3,4)\}$, and
$P_4 = \{(1,3), (3,2), (2,4)\}$.
With those definitions, the terminal reliability is defined as follows (a series connection)

$$R_{st}(G) = 1 - \prod_{k=1}^{N} q_k = 1 - \prod_{1 \le k \le N} [1 - \prod_{i, j \in k} P_{ij}] \tag{8.1}$$

For example in Figure 8.1, using (8.1) the terminal reliability of the bridge network is

$R_{st}(G) = 1 - (1 - P_{12}P_{24})(1 - P_{13}P_{34})(1 - P_{12}P_{23}P_{34})(1 - P_{13}P_{32}P_{24})$.

8.4.2   Boolean Function Decomposition Method

The method of decomposition of a Boolean function $\varphi(X)$ is very effective in some cases of network reliability. Any Boolean function can be represented as

$$\varphi(x_1,...,x_k,...,x_n) = x_k \varphi(x_1,...,1_k,...,x_n) \cup \overline{x_k} \varphi(x_1,...,0_k,...,x_n) \tag{8.2}$$

where 1_k (or 0_k) is used to show that 1 (or 0) is placed at the k-th position. If the terms of the Boolean function are interpreted as events, these two events are mutually exclusive because the first term includes x_k, and the second one includes $\overline{x_k}$. In this case, the $E\{\varphi(x)\}$ can be defined as follows

$$E\{\varphi(x_1,...,x_k,...,x_n)\} = E\{x_k \varphi(x_1,...,1_k,...,x_n)\}$$
$$+ E\{\overline{x_k} \varphi(x_1,...,0_k,...,x_n)\} \tag{8.3}$$

It can be seen that x_k and $\varphi(...1_k...)$ are independent as well as x_k and $\varphi(...0_k...)$, and thus (8.3) can finally be written as

$$E\{\varphi(x_1,...,x_k,...,x_n)\} = E\{x_k\}E\{\varphi(x_1,...,1_k,...,x_n)\}$$
$$+E\{\bar{x}_k\}E\{\varphi(x_1,...,0_k,...,x_n)\} \tag{8.4}$$

Now consider the bridge structure as an example
Suppose link 3 is chosen for decomposition. Then (8.4) can be rewritten as

$$E\{\varphi(x_1,x_2,x_3,x_4,x_5)\} = E\{x_3\}E\{\varphi(x_1,x_2,1,x_4,x_5)\}$$
$$+ E\{\bar{x}_3\}E\{\varphi(x_1,x_2,0,x_4,x_5)\}$$
$$= p_3E\{(x_1 \cup x_2)(x_4 \cup x_5)\}$$
$$+ q_3E\{x_1x_4 \cup x_2x_5\} \tag{8.5}$$

It is easy to calculate the reliability index for this network since the new structure functions under the operators E in the last row of (8.5) are functions of the reducible series-parallel and parallel-series structures. In the initial bridge structure, $x_3 = 1$ means that link 3 is absolutely reliable (it is always in the operational state). Thus, the bridge structure becomes a simple series-parallel structure. Similarly, $x_3 = 0$ means that link 3 is eliminated (it is always in a failed state). This means that the structure becomes a parallel-series structure.
Finally, $E\{\varphi(x)\}$ can be written as follows

$$E\{\varphi(x_1,x_2,x_3,x_4,x_5) = 1\} = p_3[(1-q_1q_2)(1-q_4q_5)]$$
$$+q_3[1-(1-p_1p_4)(1-p_2p_5)] \tag{8.6}$$

The same result can also be obtained with the used of direct probabilistic arguments, namely with the use of the formula

$$Pr\{\varphi(x_1,x_2,x_3,x_4,x_5) = 1\} = Pr\{\varphi(x_1,x_2,x_3,x_4,x_5)|x_3 = 1\}Pr\{x_3 = 1\}+$$
$$Pr\{\varphi(x_1,x_2,x_3,x_4,x_5)|x_3 = 0\}Pr\{x_3 = 0\} \tag{8.7}$$

Obviously, (8.6) and (8.7) are equivalent.
A Boolean function can be decomposed by any variable. In this particular example, decomposition can be done with respect to any x_k. The advantage of using the link 3 was to produce a clearer explanation.
Sometimes it is reasonable to decompose a Boolean function with respect to several variables. For example, the expression of two variables takes the form

$$\varphi(...x_k...x_j...) = x_kx_j\varphi(...1_k...1_j...)\cup \bar{x}_kx_j\varphi(...0_k...1_j...)$$
$$\cup x_k\bar{x}_j\varphi(...1_k...0_j...)\cup \bar{x}_k\bar{x}_j\varphi(...0_k...0_j...) \tag{8.8}$$

In general, this decomposition method is not practically effective. If a bridge structure is complex, the problem of choosing a unit or units with respect to which such decomposition could be reasonably done becomes very difficult. Moreover, for a complex Boolean function, an analysis of reduced functions still remains very difficult in general cases. In fact, the idea of network decomposition is nearly always represents only a nice illustrative example and not an effective tool for engineers. Thus, all of the difficulties connected with the numerical analysis of bridge structures lead to a need to find other methods.

8.4.3   Direct Enumeration Method

The direct enumeration method is the most fundamental method of calculating R_{st} (G) [2]. The bridge structure as shown in Figure 8.2 cannot be represented as a connection of parallel-series or series-parallel subsystems of independent units (links). For this example, the structure function $\varphi(x)$, where X = $(x_1, x_2, x_3, x_4, x_5)$, can be written in tabular form (Table 8.1) where all possible system states and corresponding structure function values are presented. Each Boolean variable has two possible different values, 0 or 1, so that the system can be characterized by 2^5 = 32 different states. In Table 8.1 all possible values of the variables x_1, x_2, x_3, x_4, x_5 are enumerated and denoted them as $X_1, X_2, ..., X_{32}$. Some X_k's are states of successful operation of the bridge system and some of them are not. The structure function of the bridge system can be written as

$$\varphi(x_1,...,x_5)=\varphi(X_1)\cup\varphi(X_2)\cup...\cup\varphi(X_{32})= \underset{X_k\in G}{\cup}\varphi(X_k) \qquad (8.9)$$

The probability of a system's successful operation is

$$\Pr\{\varphi(x_1,...,x_5)=1\}= E\left\{\underset{X_k\in G}{\cup}\varphi(X_k)\right\}= \sum_{X_k\in G} E\{\varphi(X_k)\} \qquad (8.10)$$

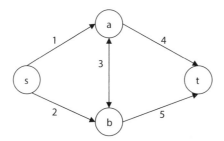

Figure 8.2 A Bridge Network.

Each vector X_k can be expressed through its component x's and x's. For example (see Table 8.1),

$$X_2 = (\bar{x}_1, x_2, x_3, x_4, x_5)$$

From Table 8.1 it is shown that the vector X_2 is a state of successful operation so that it is taken into account in (8.10). Therefore

$$E\{\varphi(X_2)\} = E\{\bar{x}_1 x_2 x_3 x_4 x_5\} = E\{\bar{x}_1\}E\{x_2\}E\{x_3\}E\{x_4\}E\{x_5\} = q_1 p_2 p_3 p_4 p_5 \quad (8.11)$$

Table 8.1 Description of the Structure Function of the Bridge Structure.

States of units					Vector	Value
x_1	x_2	x_3	x_4	x_5	X_k	$f(X_k)$
1	1	1	1	1	X_1	1
0	1	1	1	1	X_2	1
1	0	1	1	1	X_3	1
1	1	0	1	1	X_4	1
1	1	1	0	1	X_5	1
1	1	1	1	0	X_6	1
0	0	1	1	1	X_7	0
0	1	0	1	1	X_8	1
0	1	1	0	1	X_9	1
0	1	1	1	0	X_{10}	1
1	0	0	1	1	X_{11}	1
1	0	1	0	1	X_{12}	1
1	0	1	1	0	X_{13}	1
1	1	0	0	1	X_{14}	1
1	1	0	1	0	X_{15}	1
1	1	1	0	0	X_{16}	0
0	0	0	1	1	X_{17}	0
0	0	1	0	1	X_{18}	0
0	0	1	1	0	X_{19}	0
0	1	0	0	1	X_{20}	1

States of units					Vector	Value
X_1	X_2	X_3	X_4	X_5	X_k	$f(X_k)$
0	1	0	1	0	X_{21}	0
0	1	1	0	0	X_{22}	0
1	0	0	0	1	X_{23}	0
1	0	0	1	0	X_{24}	1
1	0	1	0	0	X_{25}	0
1	1	0	0	0	X_{26}	0
0	0	0	0	1	X_{27}	0
0	0	0	1	0	X_{28}	0
0	0	1	0	0	X_{29}	0
0	1	0	0	0	X_{30}	0
1	0	0	0	0	X_{31}	0
0	0	0	0	0	X_{32}	0

Based on Table 8.1, the following equation can be written

$$E\{\varphi(X)\} = E\{\varphi(X_1)\} + E\{\varphi(X_2)\} + \ldots + E\{\varphi(X_{32})\}$$

The final formula for the connectivity probability is given in two equivalent forms

$$E\{\varphi(X)\} = p^5 - 5p^4 + 2p^3 + 2p^2 \qquad (8.12)$$

$$E\{\varphi(X)\} = 1 - 2q^2 - 2q^3 + 5q^4 - 2q^5 \qquad (8.13)$$

Expression (8.13) is useful for the calculation of the reliability of a highly reliable system where $q \ll 1$. In this case, the approximation of $E\{\varphi(X)\} \cong 1 - 2q^2$.

8.4.4   Inclusion-Exclusion Method

Suppose E_i is defined to be the event that all edges in path P_i operate. Then the terminal reliability is the probability that at least one such event occurs is presented as follows

$$R_{st} (G) = Pr (E_1 \cup E_2 \cup \ldots \cup E_k) \qquad (8.14)$$

Expression (8.14) can be expanded using the principle of inclusion and exclusion [3],

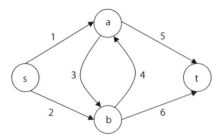

Figure 8.3 An Illustrative Network.

$$R_{st}(G) = \sum_i \Pr(E_i) - \sum_{i<j} \Pr(E_i E_j) + \sum_{i<j<l} \Pr(E_i E_j E_l) - \dots + (-1)^{k+1} \Pr(E_1 E_2 \dots E_k) \quad (8.15)$$

yielding

Using the independence assumption, each term in this expansion is easy to calculate. However, there are $2^k - 1$ terms appearing, exponential in the number of given paths.

For an example, let consider Figure 8.3 to illustrate the bridge network. There are four simple s-t paths in this network:

P_1: 1-5
P_2: 2-6
P_3: 1-3-6
P_4: 2-4-5

As a result, $\Pr(E_1) = p_1 p_5$, $\Pr(E_1 E_2) = p_1 p_2 p_5 p_6$, $\Pr(E_1 E_3) = p_1 p_3 p_5 p_6$, $\Pr(E_1 E_2 E_3) = p_1 p_2 p_3 p_5 p_6$, and so forth. Application of the inclusion-exclusion method then produces the expression

$$R_{st}(G) = (p_1 p_5 + p_2 p_6 + p_1 p_3 p_6 + p_2 p_4 p_5) - (p_1 p_2 p_5 p_6 + p_1 p_3 p_5 p_6 + p_1 p_2 p_4 p_5 +$$
$$p_1 p_2 p_3 p_6 + p_2 p_4 p_5 p_6 + p_1 p_2 p_3 p_4 p_5 p_6) + (p_1 p_2 p_3 p_5 p_6 + p_1 p_2 p_4 p_5 p_6 +$$
$$2 p_1 p_2 p_3 p_4 p_5 p_6) - (p_1 p_2 p_3 p_4 p_5 p_6)$$
$$= p_1 p_5 + p_2 p_6 + p_1 p_3 p_6 + p_2 p_4 p_5 - p_1 p_2 p_5 p_6 - p_1 p_3 p_5 p_6 - p_1 p_2 p_4 p_5 -$$
$$p_1 p_2 p_3 p_6 - p_2 p_4 p_5 p_6 + p_1 p_2 p_3 p_5 p_6 + p_1 p_2 p_4 p_5 p_6$$

Rather than the 15 possible terms appearing, cancellation has resulted in only 11 terms. In addition the coefficients of terms remaining in the reduced expression are either +1 or −1.

8.4.5   Disjoint Products Method

The disjoint products method is another way to calculate the probability of the union of events in (8.14) by decomposing $E_1 \cup E_2 \cup \dots \cup E_k$ into a union of events that are disjoint. Therefore, it can be expressed as

$$R_{st}(G) = \Pr(E_1 \cup E_2 \cup ... \cup E_k)$$
$$= \Pr(E_1 \cup \bar{E}_1 E_2 \cup \bar{E}_1 \bar{E}_2 E_3 \cup ... \cup \bar{E}_1 \bar{E}_2 \bar{E}_3 ... E_{k-1} E_k) \quad (8.16)$$

where $\bar{E}_i$ denotes the complement of event E_i. The compound events above are pairwise disjoint so the reliability can be written as follows

$$R_{st}(G) = \Pr(E_1) + \Pr(\bar{E}_1 E_2) + \Pr(\bar{E}_1 \bar{E}_2 E_3) + ... + \Pr(\bar{E}_1 \bar{E}_2 \bar{E}_3 ... E_{k-1} E_k) \quad (8.17)$$

As an example, consider the calculation of terminal reliability for the network shown in Figure 8.3, in which the paths are presented in the order:
P_1: 1-5
P_2: 1-3-6
P_3: 2-4-5
P_4: 2-6
Let the event {e operates} be denoted by e and {e fails} by $\bar{e}$. Then $\Pr(E_1)$ = Pr (15) = $p_1 p_5$ and the remaining terms are computed as

$$\Pr(\bar{E}_1 E_2) = \Pr([\bar{1} \cup \bar{5}]136) = \Pr(\bar{5}136) = p_1 p_3 q_5 p_6$$
$$\Pr(\bar{E}_1 \bar{E}_2 E_3) = \Pr([\bar{1} \cup \bar{5}][\bar{1} \cup \bar{3} \cup \bar{6}]245) = \Pr(\bar{1}[\bar{1} \cup \bar{3} \cup \bar{6}]245) = \Pr(\bar{1}245) = q_1 p_2 p_4 p_5$$
$$\Pr(\bar{E}_1 \bar{E}_2 \bar{E}_3 E_4) = \Pr([\bar{1} \cup \bar{5}][\bar{1} \cup \bar{3} \cup \bar{6}][\bar{2} \cup \bar{4} \cup \bar{5}]26) = \Pr([\bar{1} \cup \bar{5}][\bar{1} \cup \bar{3}][\bar{4} \cup \bar{5}]26)$$
$$= \Pr([\bar{1} \cup \bar{3}\bar{5}][\bar{4} \cup \bar{5}]26) = \Pr([\bar{1}\bar{4} \cup \bar{1}\bar{5} \cup \bar{3}\bar{5}]26)$$
$$= \Pr([\bar{1}\bar{4} \cup \bar{4}\bar{1}\bar{5} \cup \bar{1}\bar{3}\bar{5}]26) = \Pr(\bar{1}\bar{4}26 \cup \bar{4}\bar{1}\bar{5}26 \cup \bar{1}\bar{3}\bar{5}26)$$
$$= q_1 p_2 q_4 p_6 + q_1 p_2 p_4 q_5 p_6 + p_1 p_2 q_3 q_5 p_6$$

The final expression for the terminal reliability is then

$$R_{st}(G) = p_1 p_5 + p_1 p_3 q_5 p_6 + q_1 p_2 p_4 p_5 + q_1 p_2 q_4 p_6 + q_1 p_2 p_4 q_5 p_6 + p_1 p_2 q_3 q_5 p_6$$

If the paths were arranged in the order P_1, P_2, P_3, P_4, the calculations would be much simpler and expressed as follows

$$R_{st}(G) = p_1 p_5 + p_1 p_3 q_5 p_6 + q_1 p_2 p_6 + p_1 p_2 q_3 q_5 p_6 + q_1 p_2 p_4 p_5 q_6$$

In this case, the chosen ordering really affects on the complexity of the calculations.

8.4.6 Factoring Method

The factoring method concentrates on the state of an individual edge. A few basic rules of reduction are expressed below:

Two edges e = (i, k) and f = (i, k) joining the same two nodes in a directed network G are called parallel edges. A parallel reduction replaces two parallel edges, having reliabilities p_e and p_f, by a single edge having reliability $1 - (1 - p_e)(1 - p_f) = p_e + p_f - p_e p_f$. Two edges e = (i, j) and f = (j, k) are called series edges if these are the only two edges incident with node j. If j ≠ s, t then a series reduction replaces the two series edges by a single edge having reliability $p_e p_f$. Figure 8.4 describes these two reliability reductions, which are valid in view of the independence of edge failures. Also illustrated is a more general two-neighbor reduction, applicable when j ≠ s, t. A network G is two-terminal series parallel if it can be reduced to a single edge (s, t) by repeatedly applying series and parallel reduction. In such a case, the terminal reliability is just the reliability appearing on the final edge, and efficient algorithms exist for identifying and carrying out the appropriate reductions [4].

The reliability calculations for a given system can be decomposed into two smaller systems, G/e and G – e. The system G/e has a topological interpretation being the network obtained from G by deleting edge e and merging its endpoints. This system will not necessarily be equivalent to the network obtained from G by contracting the edge. It can be seen in the network of Figure 8.5 that using the contraction of the edge 1 produces the series-parallel network and its reliability is calculated as

$$R_{st}(G/e) = (p_2 p_5 + p_3 p_5 - p_2 p_3 p_5) + p_4 - (p_2 p_5 + p_3 p_5 - p_2 p_3 p_5) p_4$$

The system G – e is represented by the network of Figure 8.2 (assume there is only a direct path from a to b) with the edge 1 removed. Since edges 3 and 4 are then irrelevant, they can be removed and $R_{st}(G - e) = p_2 p_5$. As

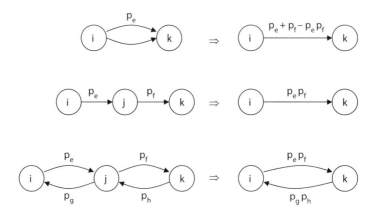

Figure 8.4 Three Probabilistic Rules of Reduction.

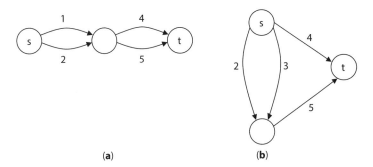

(a)   (b)

Figure 8.5 Contraction of an Edge in Fig. 3.2 (assume there is only a direct path from a to b), Using (a) e = 3 and (b) e = 1.

a result of factoring on a single edge the two-terminal reliability of G is determined as

$$R_{st}(G) = p_1 R_{st}(G/e) + (1 - p_1) R_{st}(G - e)$$
$$= P_1P_4 + P_2P_5 + P_1P_3P_5 - P_1P_2P_3P_5 - P_1P_2P_4P_5 - P_1P_3P_4P_5 + P_1P_2P_3P_4P_5$$

This example illustrates the potential advantages of decomposing a given network into smaller subnetworks, each of which may have certain probabilistic reductions, based on the network topology.

8.5   Summary

Reliability is an important measure in the network system. The all-possible pathsets among nodes are required in order to calculate the network reliability, which strongly depends on topological layout of the network. It is not an algorithmically efficient approach to compute the probabilities of all possible pathsets. For example, a complete graph on n nodes has $2^n - 1$ mincuts and n^{n-2} spanning trees. Hence, for general graphs the reliability evaluation of networks is #P complete, which means that it takes exponential time to enumerate minpaths, mincuts, or states.

In this chapter, various approaches for calculating two terminal reliability are discussed. Numerical examples of the reliability calculation for bridge network are given to demonstrate the main methods of analysis of such kinds of structure. This particular network is the simplest example of a system with a nonreducible structure that cannot be decomposed into series and parallel connections.

The two terminal reliability evaluation methods are fundamental consideration in calculating the broadcast and network (all terminal) reliability. Basically, the reliability evaluation methods described can be applied to compute the reliability in the broadcast and all terminal network. It is necessary to find the terminal path, broadcast path, and network path in order to compute those reliabilities. Chapter 9 will discuss the analysis of terminal reliability, broadcast reliability, and network reliability in the multistage interconnection networks respectively.

References

1. Shier, D. R., *Network Reliability and Algebraic Structures*, Clarendon Press, Oxford, NY, 1991.
2. Moore, E. F. and Shannon, C. E., Reliable Circuits Using Less Reliable Relays, *Journal of the Franklin Institute*, vol. 262, 191–208, 1956.
3. Satyanarayana, A. and Prabhakar, A., New Topological Formula and Rapid Algorithm for Reliability Analysis of Complex Networks, *IEEE Transactions on Reliability*, vol. 27, 82–100, 1978.
4. Politof, T. and Satyanarayana, A., Efficient Algorithms for Reliability Analysis of Planar Networks – a Survey, *IEEE Transactions on Reliability*, vol. 35, 252–259, 1986.

9

Reliability Analysis of Multistage Interconnection Networks

9.1   Reliability Analysis of Shuffle-Exchange Network with Minimal Extra Stages

In this chapter, the additional stages in Multistage Interconnection Networks (MINs) that provide more redundant paths are analyzed. A common network topology that uses a 2 x 2 basic building block such as shuffle-exchange network and its variability in terms of extra-stages will be observed. As an illustration, three types of shuffle-exchange networks [1] are compared: shuffle-exchange network (SEN), shuffle-exchange network with an additional stage (SEN+), and shuffle-exchange network with two additional stages (SEN+2). The terminal, broadcast, and network reliability of these three networks are evaluated and illustrated in graphs accordingly.

A shuffle-exchange network is a unique path MIN. Therefore, there is only a single path between a particular source (S) and a particular destination (D). In this type of network, all switching elements are critical and assumed as series connection. The switching element (SE) can either transmit the inputs straight through itself or has crossed connections.

The number of switches per stage, the number of links and the connection between stages are consistent. An eight-input/eight-output shuffle-exchange network with three stages, 12 switches (SEs), and 32 links is shown in Figure 7.11.

An N x N SEN+ is an N x N shuffle-exchange network (SEN) with an additional stage. An example of the 8 x 8 SEN+ is demonstrated by Figure 7.13. The basic idea of adding a stage to the SEN is to allow two paths for communication between each source and destination. While the paths in the first and the last stages of the SEN+ are not disjoint, the paths in the intermediate stages do traverse disjoint links. So the path redundancy in the SEN+ is achieved at the expense of one extra stage added to the SEN.

As a comparison to SEN and SEN+, a shuffle-exchange network with two additional stages (SEN+2) will be analyzed. The reliability evaluation is performed for the 8 x 8 case. In general, a SEN+2 consists of N inputs and N outputs, N/2 switching elements per stage, $(\log_2 N + 2)$ stages, and $(N)(\log_2 N + 3)$ links. The network complexity, defined as the total number of switching elements in the MIN, is $(N/2)(\log_2 N + 2)$ which for the 8 x 8 SEN+2 is 20 SEs.

9.1.1   Terminal Reliability Comparison of SEN, SEN+, and SEN+2

In this section, terminal reliability of SEN, SEN+, and SEN+2 will be compared. As an illustration, the terminal reliability of these three networks will be evaluated for the 8 x 8 case. It is noted that there is only a single path between a particular source S and a particular destination D in the 8 x 8 SEN. By adding an extra-stage to the 8 x 8 SEN, there are two terminal paths. As a matter of fact, the terminal reliability of the 8 x 8 SEN+ is higher than that of the 8 x 8 SEN.

An 8 x 8 SEN+2 consists of 8 inputs and 8 outputs, 4 switching elements per stage, 5 stages, and 48 links is demonstrated in Figure 9.1. It is observed that there are 4 terminal paths between a particular source S and a particular destination D. Therefore, it can be concluded that by adding k extra-stages to the SEN, the number of terminal paths between S and D will be 2^k. This means that a network is a $(2^k - 1)$ fault tolerant.

Assume that the position of a switching element i in stage j is represented by $SE_{i,j}$. Since there are 20 SEs in the 8 x 8 SEN+2 and 5 stages (0, 1, 2, 3, and 4), the SEs are numbered from $SE_{0,0}$, $SE_{1,0}$, ..., $SE_{2,4}$, $SE_{3,4}$. As an example, the terminal reliability between $SE_{0,0}$ and $SE_{0,4}$ in Figure 9.1 will be examined. There are 4 terminal paths between those SEs that involve the $SE_{0,1}$, $SE_{1,1}$, $SE_{0,2}$, $SE_{1,2}$, $SE_{2,2}$, $SE_{3,2}$, $SE_{0,3}$, and $SE_{2,3}$ in the intermediate stages.

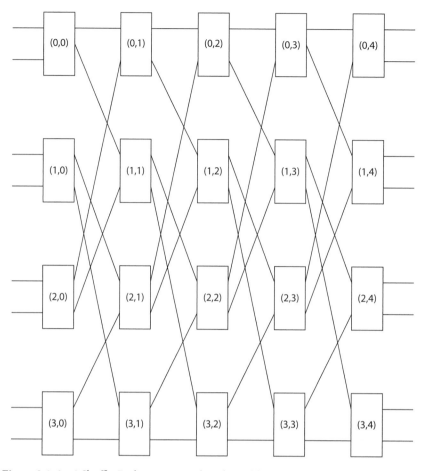

Figure 9.1 8 x 8 Shuffle-Exchange Network with 2 Additional Stages (SEN+2).

The terminal reliability calculation of the 8 x 8 SEN+2 as a function of the reliability of a switching element is summarized in Table 9.1.
The terminal reliability of the 8 x 8 SEN with 2 additional stages

$$= r^{10} + 2r^9(1\text{-}r) + 8r^8(1\text{-}r)^2 + 8r^7(1\text{-}r)^3 + 2r^7(1\text{-}r)^2 + 4r^6(1\text{-}r)^3$$
$$+ 4r^6(1\text{-}r)^2 + 4r^5(1\text{-}r)^2$$

The comparison of the SEN, SEN+, and SEN+2 for the 8 x 8 case is presented in Table 9.2. It can be seen from the results that the terminal reliability of the SEN+ > SEN > SEN+2. Therefore, it is noted that the additional terminal paths in the SEN+2 don't increase the terminal reliability of the network since the links complexity because the switching elements have more tendencies to fail the system. Hence, it can be concluded that adding one additional stage to the SEN is the most efficient way to get a higher

Table 9.1 Terminal Reliability Calculation of the 8 x 8 SEN+2.

Switching Elements								Terminal Reliability
(0,1)	(1,1)	(0,2)	(1,2)	(2,2)	(3,2)	(0,3)	(2,3)	
1	1	1	1	1	1	1	1	r^8
1	1	1	1	1	1	1	0	$2r^7(1-r)$
1	1	1	1	1	1	0	1	
1	1	1	1	1	0	1	0	
1	1	1	1	1	0	0	1	
1	1	1	1	0	1	1	0	
1	1	1	1	0	1	0	1	
1	1	1	0	1	1	1	0	
1	1	1	0	1	1	0	1	$8r^6(1-r)^2$
1	1	0	1	1	1	1	0	
1	1	0	1	1	1	0	1	
1	1	1	1	0	0	1	0	
1	1	1	1	0	0	0	1	
1	1	1	0	0	1	1	0	
1	1	1	0	0	1	0	1	
1	1	0	1	1	0	1	0	
1	1	0	1	1	0	0	1	$8r^5(1-r)^3$
1	1	0	0	1	1	1	0	
1	1	0	0	1	1	0	1	
1	1	1	0	1	0	1	X	
1	1	0	1	0	1	X	1	$2r^5(1-r)^2$
1	1	1	0	0	0	1	X	
1	1	0	1	0	0	X	1	
1	1	0	0	1	0	1	X	$4r^4(1-r)^3$
1	1	0	0	0	1	X	1	

Switching Elements								Terminal Reliability
(0,1)	(1,1)	(0,2)	(1,2)	(2,2)	(3,2)	(0,3)	(2,3)	
1	0	1	0	X	X	1	X	$2r^3 (1 - r)^2$
1	0	0	1	X	X	X	1	
1	0	1	1	X	X	1	0	$2r^4 (1 - r)^2$
1	0	1	1	X	X	0	1	
0	1	X	X	1	0	1	X	$2r^3 (1 - r)^2$
0	1	X	X	0	1	X	1	
0	1	X	X	1	1	1	0	$2r^4 (1 - r)^2$
0	1	X	X	1	1	0	1	

Table 9.2 Terminal Reliability Comparison of the 8 x 8 SEN, SEN+, and SEN+2.

SE Reliability	Terminal Reliability of the SEN	Terminal Reliability of the SEN+	Terminal Reliability of the SEN+2
0.99	0.970299	0.979712	0.924345
0.98	0.941192	0.958894	0.856787
0.96	0.884736	0.915935	0.742687
0.95	0.857375	0.893921	0.694677
0.94	0.830584	0.871628	0.651818
0.92	0.778688	0.826431	0.579273
0.90	0.729000	0.780759	0.520995

reliability. The comparison of the terminal reliability graph for these three networks is illustrated in Figure 9.2.

9.1.2 Broadcast Reliability Comparison of SEN, SEN+, and SEN+2

As an illustration, the broadcast reliability of SEN, SEN+, and SEN+2 for the 8 x 8 case will be examined. The broadcast reliability of the 8 x 8 SEN+

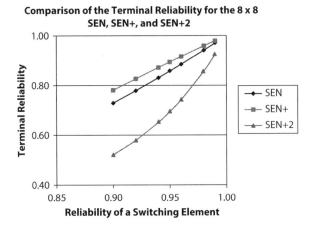

Figure 9.2 Terminal Reliability Graph of the 8 x 8 SEN, SEN+, and SEN+2.

is higher than that of the SEN since there are 2 broadcast paths in the SEN+ and only one broadcast path in the SEN.

In this section, the broadcast reliability of the 8 x 8 SEN+2 will be evaluated. Since two extra-stages are added to the SEN, there are 4 broadcast paths in the SEN+2. Table 9.3 presents the calculation of the broadcast reliability for the 8 x 8 SEN+2 that involves 10 switching elements in the intermediate stages. A particular source and all destinations are assumed to work in order to have an operational network.

The broadcast reliability of the 8 x 8 SEN with 2 additional stages

$$= r^{15} + 4r^{14}(1\text{-}r) + 20r^{13}(1\text{-}r)^2 + 32r^{12}(1\text{-}r)^3 + 16r^{11}(1\text{-}r)^4 + 10r^{11}(1\text{-}r)^2$$
$$+ 12r^{10}(1\text{-}r)^3 + 4r^9(1\text{-}r)^2$$

The results of the broadcast reliability evaluation are summarized in Table 9.4. It can be observed that the broadcast reliability of the 8 x 8 SEN+ > SEN > SEN+2. Although the number of broadcast paths in the SEN+2 is greater than that of the SEN+, the broadcast reliability of the SEN+2 is the lowest among these three networks. From this evaluation, it can be concluded that the SEN+ is the most reliable network in terms of the broadcast reliability. The comparison of broadcast reliability graph among these three networks is illustrated in Figure 9.3.

9.1.3   Network Reliability Comparison of SEN, SEN+, and SEN+2

The ability of interconnecting all sources to all destinations (network reliability) is compared in this section for the 8 x 8 SEN, SEN+, and SEN+2. It

Table 9.3 Broadcast Reliability Calculation of the 8 x 8 SEN+2.

		Switching Elements								Broadcast Reliability
(0,1)	(1,1)	(0,2)	(1,2)	(2,2)	(3,2)	(0,3)	(1,3)	(2,3)	(3,3)	
1	1	1	1	1	1	1	1	1	1	r^{10}
1	1	1	1	1	1	1	1	1	0	
1	1	1	1	1	1	1	1	0	1	$4r^9(1-r)$
1	1	1	1	1	1	1	0	1	1	
1	1	1	1	1	1	0	1	1	1	
1	1	1	1	1	1	1	1	0	0	
1	1	1	1	1	1	1	0	0	1	$4r^8(1-r)^2$
1	1	1	1	1	1	0	1	1	0	
1	1	1	1	1	1	0	0	1	1	
1	1	1	1	1	0	1	1	1	0	
1	1	1	1	1	0	1	1	0	1	$4r^8(1-r)^2$
1	1	1	1	1	0	1	0	1	1	
1	1	1	1	1	0	0	1	1	1	
1	1	1	1	1	0	1	1	0	0	
1	1	1	1	1	0	1	0	0	1	$4r^7(1-r)^3$
1	1	1	1	1	0	0	1	1	0	
1	1	1	1	1	0	0	0	1	1	
1	1	1	1	0	1	1	1	1	0	
1	1	1	1	0	1	1	1	0	1	$4r^8(1-r)^2$
1	1	1	1	0	1	1	0	1	1	
1	1	1	1	0	1	0	1	1	1	
1	1	1	1	0	1	1	1	0	0	
1	1	1	1	0	1	1	0	0	1	$4r^7(1-r)^3$
1	1	1	1	0	1	0	1	1	0	
1	1	1	1	0	1	0	0	1	1	
1	1	1	0	1	1	1	1	1	0	
1	1	1	0	1	1	1	1	0	1	$4r^8(1-r)^2$
1	1	1	0	1	1	1	0	1	1	
1	1	1	0	1	1	0	1	1	1	
1	1	1	0	1	1	1	1	0	0	
1	1	1	0	1	1	1	0	0	1	$4r^7(1-r)^3$
1	1	1	0	1	1	0	1	1	0	

(Continued)

Table 9.3 (*Cont.*)

		Switching Elements								Broadcast Reliability
(0,1)	(1,1)	(0,2)	(1,2)	(2,2)	(3,2)	(0,3)	(1,3)	(2,3)	(3,3)	
1	1	1	0	1	1	0	0	1	1	
1	1	0	1	1	1	1	1	1	0	
1	1	0	1	1	1	1	1	0	1	$4r^8 (1 - r)^2$
1	1	0	1	1	1	1	0	1	1	
1	1	0	1	1	1	0	1	1	1	
1	1	0	1	1	1	1	1	0	0	
1	1	0	1	1	1	1	0	0	1	$4r^7 (1 - r)^3$
1	1	0	1	1	1	0	1	1	0	
1	1	0	1	1	1	0	0	1	1	
1	1	1	1	0	0	1	1	1	0	
1	1	1	1	0	0	1	1	0	1	$4r^7 (1 - r)^3$
1	1	1	1	0	0	1	0	1	1	
1	1	1	1	0	0	0	1	1	1	
1	1	1	1	0	0	1	1	0	0	
1	1	1	1	0	0	1	0	0	1	$4r^6 (1 - r)^4$
1	1	1	1	0	0	0	1	1	0	
1	1	1	1	0	0	0	0	1	1	
1	1	1	0	0	1	1	1	1	0	
1	1	1	0	0	1	1	1	0	1	$4r^7 (1 - r)^3$
1	1	1	0	0	1	1	0	1	1	
1	1	1	0	0	1	0	1	1	1	
1	1	1	0	0	1	1	1	0	0	
1	1	1	0	0	1	1	0	0	1	$4r^6 (1 - r)^4$
1	1	1	0	0	1	0	1	1	0	
1	1	1	0	0	1	0	0	1	1	
1	1	0	1	1	0	1	1	1	0	
1	1	0	1	1	0	1	1	0	1	$4r^7 (1 - r)^3$
1	1	0	1	1	0	1	0	1	1	
1	1	0	1	1	0	0	1	1	1	
1	1	0	1	1	0	1	1	0	0	
1	1	0	1	1	0	1	0	0	1	$4r^6 (1 - r)^4$
1	1	0	1	1	0	0	1	1	0	
1	1	0	1	1	0	0	0	1	1	

		Switching Elements								Broadcast Reliability
(0,1)	(1,1)	(0,2)	(1,2)	(2,2)	(3,2)	(0,3)	(1,3)	(2,3)	(3,3)	
1	1	0	0	1	1	1	1	1	0	
1	1	0	0	1	1	1	1	0	1	$4r^7 (1 - r)^3$
1	1	0	0	1	1	1	0	1	1	
1	1	0	0	1	1	0	1	1	1	
1	1	0	0	1	1	1	1	0	0	
1	1	0	0	1	1	1	0	0	1	$4r^6 (1 - r)^4$
1	1	0	0	1	1	0	1	1	0	
1	1	0	0	1	1	0	0	1	1	
1	1	1	0	1	0	1	1	X	X	$2r^6 (1 - r)^2$
1	1	0	1	0	1	X	X	1	1	
1	1	1	0	0	0	1	1	X	X	
1	1	0	1	0	0	X	X	1	1	$4r^5 (1 - r)^3$
1	1	0	0	1	0	1	1	X	X	
1	1	0	0	0	1	X	X	1	1	
1	0	1	1	X	X	1	1	1	0	
1	0	1	1	X	X	1	1	0	1	$4r^6 (1 - r)^2$
1	0	1	1	X	X	1	0	1	1	
1	0	1	1	X	X	0	1	1	1	
1	0	1	1	X	X	1	1	0	0	
1	0	1	1	X	X	1	0	0	1	$4r^5 (1 - r)^3$
1	0	1	1	X	X	0	1	1	0	
1	0	1	1	X	X	0	0	1	1	
1	0	1	0	X	X	1	1	X	X	$r^4 (1 - r)^2$
1	0	0	1	X	X	X	X	1	1	$r^4 (1 - r)^2$
0	1	1	1	X	X	1	1	1	0	
0	1	1	1	X	X	1	1	0	1	$4r^6 (1 - r)^2$
0	1	1	1	X	X	1	0	1	1	
0	1	1	1	X	X	0	1	1	1	
0	1	1	1	X	X	1	1	0	0	
0	1	1	1	X	X	1	0	0	1	$4r^5 (1 - r)^3$
0	1	1	1	X	X	0	1	1	0	
0	1	1	1	X	X	0	0	1	1	
0	1	1	0	X	X	1	1	X	X	$r^4 (1 - r)^2$
0	1	0	1	X	X	X	X	1	1	$r^4 (1 - r)^2$

Table 9.4 Broadcast Reliability Comparison of the 8 x 8 SEN, SEN+, and SEN+2.

SE Reliability	Broadcast Reliability of the SEN	Broadcast Reliability of the SEN+	Broadcast Reliability of the SEN+2
0.99	0.932065	0.950334	0.897863
0.98	0.868126	0.901462	0.809831
0.96	0.751447	0.806756	0.667692
0.95	0.698337	0.761192	0.610132
0.94	0.648478	0.716965	0.559696
0.92	0.557847	0.632844	0.475794
0.90	0.478297	0.554872	0.408837

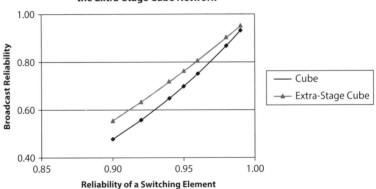

Figure 9.3 Broadcast Reliability Graph of the 8 x 8 SEN, SEN+, and SEN+2.

is noted that the network reliability of the 8 x 8 SEN+ is much higher than that of the 8 x 8 SEN in all reliability zones of switching elements.

Table 9.5 presents the calculation of the network reliability of the SEN+2 for 8 x 8 case. All switching elements in stage 0 and 4 are assumed to work for the SEN+2 system to be operational. Therefore, from reliability point of view, these switching elements are in series so that the reliability for stage 0 and 4 is r^8. Then, by conditioning at stage 1 and proceeding with all possible combinations of paths through stage 3, the network reliability of the

Table 9.5 Network Reliability Calculation of the 8 x 8 SEN+2.

| | Switching Elements | | | | | | | | | | | | Network Reliability |
(0,1)	(1,1)	(2,1)	(3,1)	(0,2)	(1,2)	(2,2)	(3,2)	(0,3)	(1,3)	(2,3)	(3,3)	
1	1	1	1	1	1	1	1	1	1	1	1	r^{12}
1	1	1	1	1	1	1	1	1	1	1	0	$4r^{11}(1-r)$
1	1	1	1	1	1	1	1	1	1	0	0	$4r^{10}(1-r)^2$
1	1	1	1	1	1	1	0	1	1	1	0	$16r^{10}(1-r)^2$
1	1	1	1	1	1	1	0	1	1	0	0	$16r^{9}(1-r)^3$
1	1	1	1	1	1	0	0	1	1	1	0	$16r^{9}(1-r)^3$
1	1	1	1	1	1	0	0	1	1	0	0	$16r^{8}(1-r)^4$
1	1	1	1	1	0	1	0	1	1	X	X	$2r^{8}(1-r)^2$
1	1	1	1	1	0	0	0	1	1	X	X	$4r^{7}(1-r)^3$
1	1	1	0	1	1	1	1	1	1	1	0	$16r^{10}(1-r)^2$
1	1	1	0	1	1	1	1	1	1	0	0	$16r^{9}(1-r)^3$
1	1	1	0	1	1	1	0	1	1	1	0	$64r^{9}(1-r)^3$
1	1	1	0	1	1	1	0	1	1	0	0	$64r^{8}(1-r)^4$
1	1	1	0	1	1	0	0	1	1	1	0	$48r^{8}(1-r)^4$

(Continued)

Table 9.5 (Cont.)

(0,1)	(1,1)	(2,1)	(3,1)	(0,2)	(1,2)	(2,2)	(3,2)	(0,3)	(1,3)	(2,3)	(3,3)	Network Reliability
					Switching Elements							
1	1	1	0	1	1	0	0	1	1	0	0	$48r^7(1-r)^5$
1	1	1	0	1	0	1	0	1	1	X	X	$8r^7(1-r)^3$
1	1	1	0	1	0	0	0	1	1	X	X	$2r^6(1-r)^4$
1	0	1	0	1	1	X	X	1	1	1	0	$8r^7(1-r)^3$
1	0	1	0	1	1	X	X	1	1	0	0	$8r^6(1-r)^4$
1	0	1	0	1	0	X	X	1	1	X	X	$2r^5(1-r)^3$
1	0	1	0	0	1	X	X	X	X	1	1	$2r^5(1-r)^3$
1	0	0	1	1	1	1	1	1	1	1	0	$8r^9(1-r)^3$
1	0	0	1	1	1	1	1	1	1	0	0	$8r^8(1-r)^4$
1	0	0	1	1	1	1	0	1	1	1	0	$32r^8(1-r)^4$
1	0	0	1	1	1	1	0	1	1	0	0	$32r^7(1-r)^5$
1	0	0	1	1	1	0	0	1	1	1	0	$16r^7(1-r)^5$
1	0	0	1	1	1	0	0	1	1	0	0	$16r^6(1-r)^6$
1	0	0	1	1	0	1	0	1	1	X	X	$4r^6(1-r)^4$

8 x 8 SEN+2 can be examined. For this calculation, a k out of n redundancy principle is applied in which there are at least k out of n components to function for the system to work.

The network reliability of the 8 x 8 SEN with 2 additional stages

$$= r^{20} + 4r^{19}(1\text{-}r) + 36r^{18}(1\text{-}r)^2 + 120r^{17}(1\text{-}r)^3 + 168r^{16}(1\text{-}r)^4 + 2r^{16}(1\text{-}r)^2 + 96r^{15}(1\text{-}r)^5 + 20r^{15}(1\text{-}r)^3 + 16r^{14}(1\text{-}r)^6 + 14r^{14}(1\text{-}r)^4 + 4r^{13}(1\text{-}r)^3$$

The comparison of the network reliability evaluation of the SEN, SEN+, and SEN+2 for the 8 x 8 case is summarized in Table 9.6. The comparison of the network reliability graph for these three networks is also illustrated in Figure 9.4.

It can be observed from the table that the network reliability of the 8 x 8 SEN+ > SEN > SEN+2. This fact again proves that adding an additional stage to the SEN is the most reliable shuffle-exchange network.

9.1.4   Concluding Remarks

In this chapter, three types of shuffle-exchange networks are compared: shuffle-exchange network (SEN), shuffle-exchange network with an additional stage (SEN+), and shuffle-exchange network with two additional stages (SEN+2). The terminal, broadcast, and network reliability of these three networks are evaluated and illustrated in graphs accordingly.

In general, a SEN+2 consists of N inputs and N outputs, N/2 switching elements per stage, $(\log_2 N + 2)$ stages, and $(N) (\log_2 N + 3)$ links. The

Table 9.6 Network Reliability Comparison of the 8 x 8 SEN, SEN+, and SEN+2.

SE Reliability	Network Reliability of the SEN	Network Reliability of the SEN+	Network Reliability of the SEN+2
0.99	0.886385	0.921659	0.854252
0.98	0.784717	0.846842	0.733541
0.96	0.612710	0.708630	0.549891
0.95	0.540360	0.645470	0.480112
0.94	0.475920	0.586322	0.421465
0.92	0.367666	0.479906	0.329657
0.90	0.282430	0.388708	0.262133

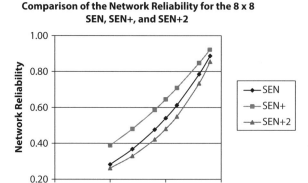

Figure 9.4 Network Reliability Graph of the 8 x 8 SEN, SEN+, and SEN+2..

network complexity, defined as the total number of switching elements in the MIN, is $(N/2)$ $(\log_2 N + 2)$ which for the 8 x 8 SEN+2 is 20 SEs.

It can be concluded that by adding k extra-stages to the SEN, the number of terminal paths between S and D will be 2^k. This condition is also valid for broadcast paths. The additional k stages will create 2^k broadcast paths between a particular source and all destinations. It means that a shuffle-exchange network is a $(2^k - 1)$ fault tolerant. Therefore, for the 8 x 8 case the terminal paths and the broadcast paths of the SEN+ and SEN+2 are 2 and 4 respectively.

It can be seen from the results in Table 9.2 that the terminal reliability of the SEN+ > SEN > SEN+2. Therefore, it is noted that the additional terminal paths in the SEN+2 don't increase the terminal reliability of the network since the links complexity because the switching elements have more tendencies to fail the system.

Table 9.4 shows that the broadcast reliability of the 8 x 8 SEN+ > SEN > SEN+2. Although the number of broadcast paths in the SEN+2 is greater than that of the SEN+, the broadcast reliability of the SEN+2 is the lowest among these three networks. From this evaluation, it can be concluded that the SEN+ is the most reliable network in terms of the broadcast reliability.

It can be observed from the Table 9.6 that the network reliability of the 8 x 8 SEN+ > SEN > SEN+2. This fact again proves that adding an additional stage to the SEN is the most reliable shuffle-exchange network since the SEN+ has the highest terminal, broadcast, and network reliability comparing to the original shuffle-exchange network (SEN) and shuffle-exchange network with two additional stages (SEN+2).

9.2   Terminal Reliability Improvement in Modified Shuffle-Exchange Network

In this chapter, a modified shuffle-exchange network is introduced. This network is constructed by 1 x 2 switching elements (SEs) at the input stage, 2 x 2 SEs at the intermediate stages, and 2 x 1 SEs at the output stage [2].

The shuffle-exchange multistage interconnection network (SEN) is one network in a large class of topologically equivalent MINs that includes the omega, indirect binary n-cube, baseline, and generalized cube. Figure 7.11 is an example of an 8 x 8 SEN. Each switching element (SE), the basic building block of a SEN, can be viewed as a 2 x 2 SEN. The SE can either transmit the inputs straight through itself or has crossed connections.

A SEN has $N = 2^n$ inputs, termed sources (S), and 2^n outputs termed destinations (D). There is a unique path between each source-destination pair. The SEN has n stages and each stage has N/2 switching elements. The network complexity, defined as the total number of switching elements in the MIN, is $(N/2) (\log_2 N)$ which for the 8 x 8 SEN is 12 switching elements.

A modified shuffle-exchange network (MODSEN) consists of N inputs, N outputs, $(\log_2 N) + 2$ stages, and each stage has N switching elements. In this type of network, the network complexity is $(N) [(\log_2 N) + 2]$, which for the 8 x 8 MODSEN is 40 switching elements. There are two paths between each source-destination pair so that the MODSEN is 1-fault tolerant network.

9.2.1   Terminal Reliability of Shuffle-Exchange Network (SEN)

The reliability measure of particular interest to demonstrate the performance of a network is terminal reliability. Terminal reliability, generally used as a measure of robustness of a MIN, is the probability of existence of at least one fault free path between a designated pair of input (s) and output (t) terminals (two-terminal). This is denoted by $R_{st} (G)$, where G is the network representing the system. G can be directed or undirected. If G is directed, there should at least be one directed path between s and t.

In this section, the terminal reliability analysis will be performed. A network is operational as long as every input can communicate with every output. It is assumed that the switching elements that compose the network are identical and have independent times to failure. Also, they are either in fully operational state or failed.

The 4 x 4 SEN has four SEs, two in each of two stages, which is shown in Figure 9.5.

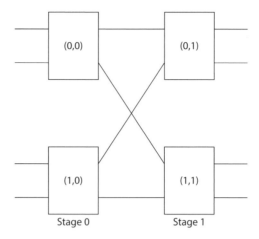

Figure 9.5 4 x 4 Shuffle-Exchange Network (SEN).

Since the SEN is a unique-path MIN, the failure of any switch in a terminal path will cause system failure. Therefore, from the reliability point of view, there are $\log_2 N$ switching elements in series. Hence, if $r_{SE}(t)$ is the time-dependent reliability of the basic SE, the terminal reliability of an N x N SEN is given by:

$$R_{st}(t) = [r_{SE}(t)]^{\log_2 N} \tag{9.1}$$

In the 4 x 4 SEN, it is clear that the terminal reliability is $R_{st}(t) = [r_{SE}(t)]^2$.

Table 9.7 summarizes the terminal reliability evaluation of shuffle-exchange network in the size of 4 x 4, 8 x 8, 16 x 16, and 32 x 32. The terminal reliability of SEN in the size 8 x 8, 16 x 16, and 32 x 32 can be calculated based on the above formula, which are $[r_{SE}(t)]^3$, $[r_{SE}(t)]^4$, and $[r_{SE}(t)]^5$ respectively. As the network size increases, the terminal reliability of SEN as a function of the reliability of a SE ranging from 0.90 – 0.99 decreases. The number of intermediate stages leads to more elements subject to failure in SEN. The terminal reliability of different SEN sizes is illustrated in Figure 9.6.

9.2.2   Terminal Reliability of Modified Shuffle-Exchange Network (MODSEN)

A modified shuffle-exchange network is two-paths MIN. In this network, there are two terminal paths between each source and each destination. In general, from the reliability point of view, it is assumed that the switching elements at the input and output stage must be operational and at least one

Table 9.7 Terminal Reliability Evaluation of Shuffle-Exchange Network (SEN).

Reliability of a SE	Terminal Reliability of SEN			
	4 x 4	8 x 8	16 x 16	32 x 32
0.99	0.9801	0.9703	0.9606	0.9510
0.98	0.9604	0.9412	0.9224	0.9039
0.96	0.9216	0.8847	0.8493	0.8154
0.95	0.9025	0.8574	0.8145	0.7738
0.94	0.8836	0.8306	0.7807	0.7339
0.92	0.8464	0.7787	0.7164	0.6591
0.90	0.8100	0.7290	0.6561	0.5905

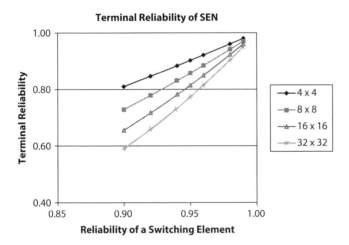

Figure 9.6 Terminal Reliability Graph of Shuffle-Exchange Network (SEN).

terminal path must be available in order to have a connection between an input and an output.

As an example, the 4 x 4 MODSEN is illustrated in Figure 9.7. This network has 4 inputs, 4 outputs, 4 stages, and 4 switching elements in each stage. The network complexity defined as the total number of switching elements for the 4 x 4 MODSEN is 16 switching elements.

The terminal reliability of the 4 x 4 MODSEN can be computed as a series structure between the input stage, the intermediate stages, and the output stage. The intermediate stages itself is a parallel-series structure, which consist of $2\log_2 N$ switching elements. The terminal paths for the 4

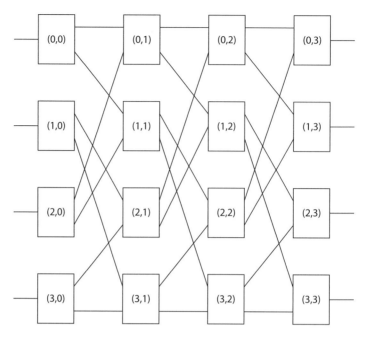

Figure 9.7   4 x 4 Modified Shuffle-Exchange Network (MODSEN).

x 4 MODSEN is shown in Figure 9.8. Hence, the terminal reliability of this network can be calculated as $R_{st}(t) = 2[r_{SE}(t)]^4 - [r_{SE}(t)]^6$.

In general, the reliability of the intermediate stages can be calculated as $2[r_{SE}(t)]^{\log_2 N} - [r_{SE}(t)]^{2\log_2 N}$. Therefore, by assuming the switching elements at the input and the output stage operational in order to have a connection between each source and each destination, the terminal reliability of an N x N MODSEN can be calculated as follows:

$$R_{st}(t) = [r_{SE}(t)]^2 \{2[r_{SE}(t)]^{\log_2 N} - [r_{SE}(t)]^{2\log_2 N}\}$$
$$= 2[r_{SE}(t)]^{(\log_2 N) + 2} - [r_{SE}(t)]^{(2\log_2 N) + 2} \qquad (9.2)$$

The terminal reliability of the MODSEN in the size of 8 x 8, 16 x 16, and 32 x 32 can be computed based on the equation above, which are $2[r_{SE}(t)]^5 - [r_{SE}(t)]^8$, $2[r_{SE}(t)]^6 - [r_{SE}(t)]^{10}$, and $2[r_{SE}(t)]^7 - [r_{SE}(t)]^{12}$ respectively. Table 9.8 shows the terminal reliability evaluation of the MODSEN for various sizes and illustrated in Figure 9.9.

It can be observed from the above figure that the terminal reliability of the MODSEN is lower as the reliability of a switching element decreases. In high reliability zone, the terminal reliability of the MODSEN for various sizes is not significantly different.

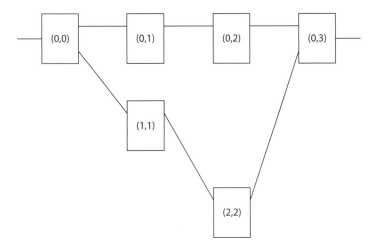

Figure 9.8 Terminal Paths of the 4 x 4 MODSEN.

Table 9.8 Terminal Reliability Evaluation of Modified Shuffle-Exchange Network.

	Terminal Reliability of MODSEN			
Reliability of a SE	**4 x 4**	**8 x 8**	**16 x 16**	**32 x 32**
0.99	0.9797	0.9792	0.9786	0.9777
0.98	0.9589	0.9571	0.9546	0.9515
0.96	0.9159	0.9094	0.9007	0.8902
0.95	0.8939	0.8841	0.8714	0.8563
0.94	0.8716	0.8582	0.8411	0.8210
0.92	0.8264	0.8049	0.7783	0.7480
0.90	0.7808	0.7505	0.7142	0.6742

9.2.3   Comparison of the Networks

By examining the results for terminal reliability, it can be seen that the 4 x 4 MODSEN is less reliable than the corresponding SEN. The MODSEN is not more reliable than the corresponding SEN unless the number of components at the intermediate stages is sufficiently larger than the number of components at the first and last stage combined. For $N \geq 8$ the MODSEN is strictly more reliable than the SEN.

As an illustration, the SEN and MODSEN for the 32 x 32 case will be compared. Table 9.9 presents the comparison of terminal reliability

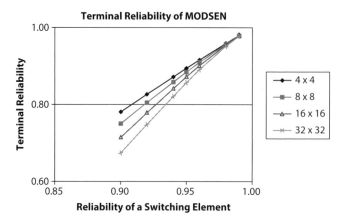

Figure 9.9 Terminal Reliability Graph of Modified Shuffle-Exchange Network.

Table 9.9 Comparison of Terminal Reliability Evaluation Between the SEN and MODSEN for the 32 x 32 Case.

Reliability of a SE	Terminal SEN	Reliability of MODSEN
0.99	0.9510	0.9777
0.98	0.9039	0.9515
0.96	0.8154	0.8902
0.95	0.7738	0.8563
0.94	0.7339	0.8210
0.92	0.6591	0.7480
0.90	0.5905	0.6742

between the SEN and MODSEN for the 32 x 32 case. It is noted that the terminal reliability of the MODSEN is higher than that of the SEN. As the reliability of a SE decreases, the terminal reliability for these networks also decreases. Figure 9.10 illustrates the terminal reliability comparison between these networks in a graph.

9.2.4   Conclusion

In this chapter, terminal reliability evaluation between Shuffle-Exchange Network (SEN) and Modified Shuffle-Exchange Network (MODSEN) is conducted. The MODSEN is constructed by 1 x 2 switching elements (SEs)

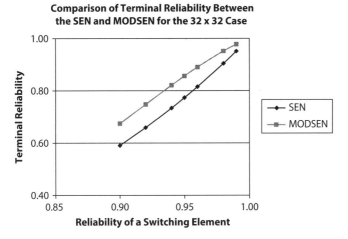

Figure 9.10 Comparison of Terminal Reliability Graph. Between the SEN and MODSEN for the 32 x 32 Case.

at the input stage, 2 x 2 SEs at the intermediate stages, and 2 x 1 SEs at the output stage. The MODSEN consists of N inputs, N outputs, $(\log_2 N) + 2$ stages, and each stage has N switching elements.

By changing the switch size at the input and output stage and adding two additional stages to the corresponding SEN, the MODSEN has two terminal paths between each source and each destination. In this case, the MODSEN is categorized as a 1-fault tolerant network that has one redundant path in the network.

It can be observed from the results that the terminal reliability of the MODSEN is higher than that of the SEN. As the reliability of a SE decreases, the terminal reliability for these networks also decreases. In high reliability zone, the terminal reliability of the MODSEN for various sizes is not significantly different.

The 4 x 4 MODSEN is less reliable than the corresponding SEN. The MODSEN is not more reliable than the corresponding SEN unless the number of components at the intermediate stages is sufficiently larger than the number of components at the first and last stage combined. For $N \geq 8$ the MODSEN is strictly more reliable than the SEN. Therefore, the MODSEN is much better than the corresponding SEN in large size of networks.

9.3   Reliability Bounds for Large MINs

To derive the exact reliability expressions for large MINs can become rather complex. As network size increases, the reliability bounds could be used to estimate the reliability of the networks. Upper and lower bounds reliability will be determined to estimate network reliability [3-6].

Lower bound reliability is the minimum probability that the system will be operational for a specified time. Upper bound reliability presents an optimistic view of probability that the system will work at some specified time, which is not the center of attention in terms of reliability point of view. If the lower bound reliability provides sufficient assurance that the system will be operational at some specified time, then no further effort for obtaining the exact reliability expression is necessary. As examples, the derivation of the lower and upper bounds reliability expressions of the extra-stage cube network and the gamma network will be demonstrated.

9.3.1   Lower Bound Reliability of the Extra-Stage Cube Network

It can be observed that to obtain a lower bound reliability of the extra-stage cube network, as many as one-half of the switching elements can be failed at the intermediate stages, and the network remains operational. For the 8 x 8 case, 4 switching elements can be failed at stage 1 and 2. Figure 9.11 shows that $SE_{1,2}$, $SE_{3,2}$, $SE_{1,1}$, $SE_{3,1}$ can be failed and yet the network remains operational.

Since one-half of the SEs can be failed at the intermediate stages, the intermediate stages can be modeled as a parallel-series system, which consists of a parallel arrangement of two series subsystem, each with (N/4) $[(\log_2 N) - 1]$ switches as illustrated in Figure 9.12.

$$R_{lb}(t) = [r_{SE}(t)]^N \left[1 - [1 - r_{SE}(t)^{N/4[(\log_2 N)-1]}]^2 \right] \qquad (9.3)$$

Based on the reliability block diagram as shown above, the lower bound reliability of the extra-stage cube network can be computed. There are three subsystems in the diagram: the first and the last are series subsystems and the middle subsystem is a parallel-series subsystem. Hence, the lower bound reliability expression is:

As an illustration, the lower bound reliability of the extra-stage cube network for the 8 x 8, 16 x 16, 32 x 32, 64 x 64, and 128 x 128 cases will be demonstrated. Table 9.10 presents the lower bound reliability evaluation for those networks. The lower bound reliability graph is illustrated in Figure 9.13.

It can be observed from the graph that as network size increases, the lower bound reliability decreases. This is due to an increment in the number of switches in series, where the input and output stages consist of N switches in series and the intermediate stages have N/4 $[(\log_2 N) - 1]$ switches in series.

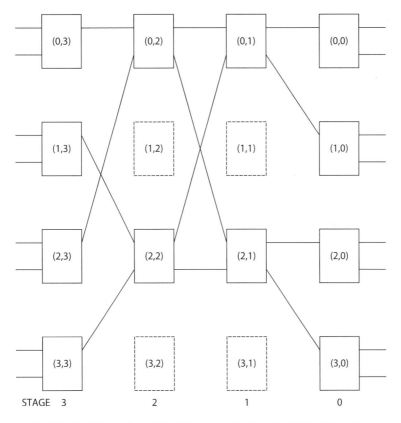

Figure 9.11 The 8 x 8 Extra-Stage Cube Network with One-Half of the SEs at the Intermediate Stages Failed.

9.3.2   Upper Bound Reliability of the Extra-Stage Cube Network

$$R_{ub}(t) = [r_{SE}(t)]^{N}[1-(1-r_{SE}(t))^{N/2}]^{(\log_2 N)-1} \qquad (9.4)$$

Upper bound reliability presents an optimistic view that the system will be operational at some specified time. To obtain an upper bound reliability of the extra-stage cube network, it is assumed that the system consisted of $(\log_2 N) + 1$ subsystems as illustrated in Figure 9.14. The first and last subsystems are each composed of $N/2$ SEs in series, and the intermediate subsystems are composed of SEs arranged in parallel. In this case, the system is $(N/2 - 1)$-fault tolerant since there are $N/2$ SEs in each of the intermediate stages. This condition will definitely overestimate the reliability because there is only one SE is needed in each of the intermediate stages to make

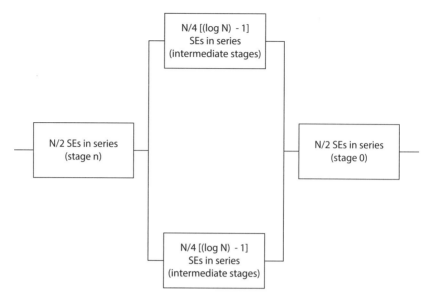

Figure 9.12 Reliability Block Diagram of the Lower Bound for the Extra-Stage Cube Network.

Table 9.10 Lower Bound Reliability Evaluation for the Extra-Stage Cube Network.

Reliability of a SE	Lower Bound Reliability of ESC Network				
	8 x 8	16 x 16	32 x 32	64 x 64	128 x 128
0.999	0.992012	0.983979	0.967530	0.932425	0.464311
0.998	0.984049	0.967930	0.934333	0.860473	0.170166
0.996	0.968199	0.935817	0.866882	0.715521	0.018335
0.995	0.960314	0.919786	0.833094	0.646383	0.005754
0.994	0.952457	0.903793	0.799520	0.581008	0.001780
0.992	0.936826	0.871976	0.733617	0.463657	0.000165
0.990	0.921312	0.840467	0.670146	0.365168	0.000015

connections for all source-destination pairs. Hence, the upper bound reliability can be calculated as:

Table 9.11 presents the upper bound reliability evaluation of the extra-stage cube network for different sizes. As network size increases, the upper bound reliability decreases as shown in Figure 9.15.

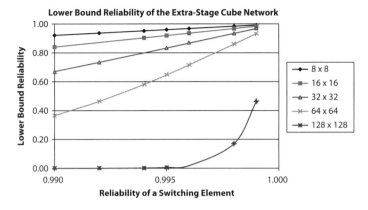

Figure 9.13 Lower Bound Reliability Graph for the Extra-Stage Cube Network.

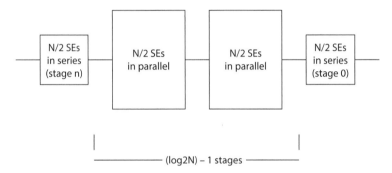

Figure 9.14 Reliability Block Diagram of the Upper Bound. for the Extra-Stage Cube Network.

Table 9.11 Upper Bound Reliability Evaluation for the Extra-Stage Cube Network.

Reliability of a SE	Upper Bound Reliability of ESC Network				
	8 x 8	**16 x 16**	**32 x 32**	**64 x 64**	**128 x 128**
0.999	0.992028	0.984119	0.968491	0.937975	0.599142
0.998	0.984112	0.968476	0.937945	0.879741	0.358787
0.996	0.968444	0.937885	0.879628	0.773745	0.128464
0.995	0.960693	0.922931	0.851802	0.725566	0.076810
0.994	0.952996	0.908201	0.824830	0.680344	0.045902
0.992	0.937764	0.879401	0.773345	0.598063	0.016367
0.990	0.922745	0.851458	0.724980	0.525596	0.005824

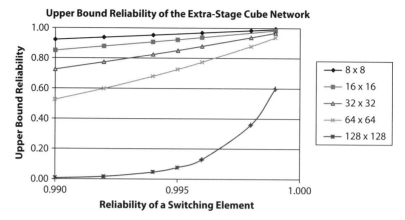

Figure 9.15 Upper Bound Reliability Graph for the Extra-Stage Cube Network.

9.3.3 Comparison of the Bounds with the Exact Reliability of the Extra-Stage Cube Network

Table 9.12 compares the upper (optimistic) and lower (conservative) bounds reliability for an 8 x 8 extra-stage cube network with the exact reliability expression.

As can be observed from the results, the lower bound reliability closely approximates the exact reliability of the extra-stage cube network. The lower bound provides sufficient assurance that the system will be operational at some specified time, so that it can be concluded that the lower bound reliability expression derived before is a reasonable approximation to the actual reliability of the extra-stage cube network. Figure 9.16 shows the comparison of the upper and lower bounds with the exact reliability of the 8 x 8 extra-stage cube network.

9.3.4 Lower Bound Reliability of the Gamma Network

To obtain a lower bound reliability of the gamma network, at most two-third of the switching elements can fail at stages 1 (rounded off to the lower integer) to (n − 2) and as many as one-half of the switching elements can fail at stage (n − 1), and the network remains operational. Therefore, the intermediate stages can be modeled as two parallel-series systems, which consist of parallel arrangement of series subsystems as illustrated in Figure 9.17.

Based on the reliability block diagram as shown below, the lower bound reliability of the gamma network can be computed. There are four subsystems in the diagram: the first and the last are series subsystems and the middle subsystems are parallel-series subsystems.

Table 9.12 Comparison of the Upper and Lower Bounds Evaluation with the Exact Reliability of the 8 x 8 Extra-Stage Cube Network.

Reliability of A SE	Reliability of the ESC		Network
	LB	Exact	UB
0.999	0.992012	0.992016	0.992028
0.998	0.984049	0.984065	0.984112
0.996	0.968199	0.968260	0.968444
0.995	0.960314	0.960408	0.960693
0.994	0.952457	0.952589	0.952996
0.992	0.936826	0.937055	0.937764
0.990	0.921312	0.921659	0.922745

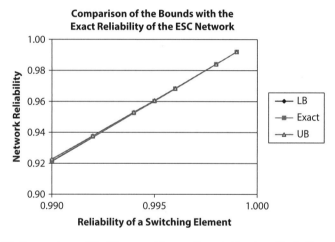

Figure 9.16 Comparison of the Upper and Lower Bounds Graph. with the Exact Reliability of the 8 x 8 Extra-Stage Cube Network

Hence, the lower bound reliability expression is:

$$R_{lb}(t) = [r_{SE}(t)]^{2N} \left[1 - [1 - r_{SE}(t)^{N/3[(\log_2 N)-2]}]^3 \right] \left[1 - [1 - r_{SE}(t)^{N/2}]^2 \right] \quad (9.5)$$

As examples, the lower bound reliability of the gamma network for the 8 x 8, 16 x 16, 32 x 32, 64 x 64, and 128 x 128 cases will be demonstrated. Table 9.13 presents the lower bound reliability evaluation for these networks. The lower bound reliability graph is illustrated in Figure 9.18.

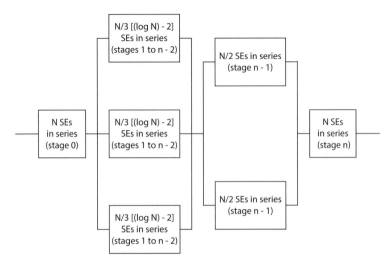

Figure 9.17　Reliability Block Diagram of the Lower Bound for the Gamma Network.

Table 9.13　Lower Bound Reliability Evaluation for the Gamma Network.

Reliability of a SE	Lower Bound Reliability of Gamma Network				
	8 x 8	16 x 16	32 x 32	64 x 64	128 x 128
0.999	0.976274	0.953110	0.908392	0.824775	0.676165
0.998	0.953088	0.908368	0.824951	0.678233	0.444114
0.996	0.908288	0.824929	0.679420	0.451968	0.173841
0.995	0.886651	0.786044	0.616027	0.365872	0.104570
0.994	0.865509	0.748931	0.558152	0.294508	0.061684
0.992	0.824662	0.679704	0.457124	0.187794	0.020550
0.990	0.785664	0.616642	0.373121	0.117473	0.006577

It can be observed from the graph that as network size increases, the lower bound reliability decreases. This is due to an increment in the number of switches in series, where the input and output stages consist of 2N switches in series and the intermediate stages have $N/3 \ [(\log_2 N) - 2]$ and $N/2$ switches in series.

9.3.5　Upper Bound Reliability of the Gamma Network

To obtain an upper bound reliability of the gamma network, it is assumed that the system consisted of $(\log_2 N) + 1$ subsystems. Figure 9.19 illustrates

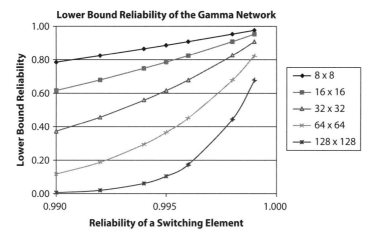

Figure 9.18 Lower Bound Reliability Graph for the Gamma Network.

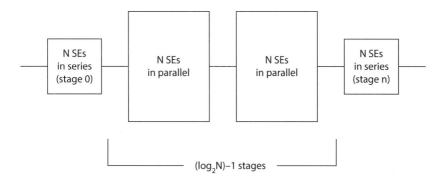

Figure 9.19 Reliability Block Diagram of the Upper Bound for the Gamma Network.

the reliability block diagram of the upper bound for the gamma network. The first and last subsystems are each composed of N SEs in series, and the intermediate subsystems are composed of SEs arranged in parallel. In this case, the system is (N − 1)-fault tolerant since there are N SEs in each of the intermediate stages. This condition will definitely overestimate the reliability because there is only one SE is needed in each of the intermediate stages to make connections for all source-destination pairs. Hence, the upper bound reliability can be calculated as:

$$R_{ub}(t) = [r_{SE}(t)]^{2N}[1 - (1 - r_{SE}(t))^N]^{(\log_2 N)-1} \qquad (9.6)$$

Table 9.14 presents the upper bound reliability evaluation of the gamma network for different sizes. As network size increases, the upper bound reliability decreases as shown in Figure 9.20.

Table 9.14 Upper Bound Reliability Evaluation for the Gamma Network.

Reliability of a SE	Upper Bound Reliability of Gamma Network				
	8 x 8	16 x 16	32 x 32	64 x 64	128 x 128
0.999	0.984119	0.968491	0.937975	0.879797	0.774043
0.998	0.968476	0.937945	0.879741	0.773944	0.598989
0.996	0.937885	0.879628	0.773745	0.598681	0.358419
0.995	0.922931	0.851802	0.725566	0.526447	0.277146
0.994	0.908201	0.824830	0.680344	0.462868	0.214247
0.992	0.879401	0.773345	0.598063	0.357679	0.127935
0.990	0.851458	0.724980	0.525596	0.276252	0.076315

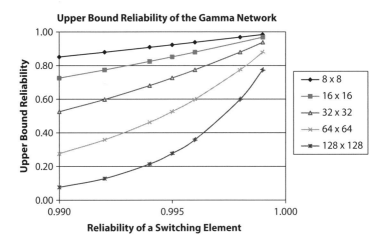

Figure 9.20 Upper Bound Reliability Graph for the Gamma Network.

9.3.6   Comparison of the Bounds with the Exact Reliability of the Gamma Network

Table 9.15 compares the upper (optimistic) and lower (conservative) bounds reliability for an 8 x 8 gamma network with the derived exact reliability expression

As can be seen from the results, the lower bound reliability closely approximates the exact reliability of the gamma network. The lower bound provides sufficient assurance that the system will be operational at some

Table 9.15 Comparison of the Upper and Lower Bounds Evaluation with the Exact Reliability of the 8 x 8 Gamma Network.

Reliability of a SE	Reliability of the Gamma Network		
	LB	Exact	UB
0.999	0.976274	0.976305	0.984119
0.998	0.953088	0.953210	0.968476
0.996	0.908288	0.908752	0.937885
0.995	0.886651	0.887359	0.922931
0.994	0.865509	0.866503	0.908201
0.992	0.824662	0.826346	0.879401
0.990	0.785664	0.788168	0.851458

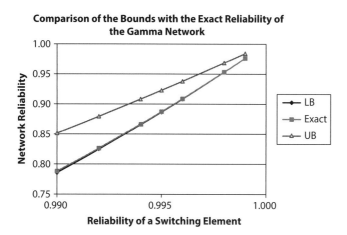

Figure 9.21 Comparison of the Upper and Lower Bounds Graph with the Exact Reliability of the 8 x 8 Gamma Network.

specified time, so that it can be concluded that the lower bound reliability expression derived above is a reasonable approximation to the actual reliability of the gamma network.

The reliability of the extra-stage cube network is higher than that of the gamma network since more switching elements and larger network complexity in a gamma network lead to more elements subject to failure. Figure 9.21 shows the comparison of the upper and lower bounds with the exact reliability of the 8 x 8 gamma network.

9.3.7   Conclusion

In this chapter, the reliability bounds of an extra-stage cube network and a gamma network are derived. The reliability block diagrams for a lower and an upper bound are also presented in order to calculate the reliability bounds. As an illustration, the reliability bounds are compared to the exact reliability for the case of the 8 x 8 extra-stage cube network and the 8 x 8 gamma network.

As can be observed from the results, the lower bound reliability closely approximates the exact reliability of the extra-stage cube network. The lower bound provides sufficient assurance that the system will be operational at some specified time, so that it can be concluded that the lower bound reliability expression derived before is a reasonable approximation to the actual reliability of the extra-stage cube network.

On the other hand, the lower bound reliability of the gamma network also closely approximates its exact reliability. The reliability of the 8 x 8 gamma network decreases as the reliability of a switching element decreases. For larger network sizes, the exact network reliability can be estimated using the lower bound reliability.

The reliability of the extra-stage cube network is higher than that of the gamma network since more switching elements and larger network complexity in a gamma network lead to more elements subject to failure.

References

1. Gunawan, I., Reliability Analysis of Shuffle-Exchange Network Systems, *Reliability Engineering and System Safety*, Vol. 93, No. 2, 271–276, 2008.
2. Fard, N. S. and Gunawan, I., Terminal Reliability Improvement of Shuffle-Exchange Network Systems, *International Journal of Reliability, Quality and Safety Engineering*, Vol. 12, No. 1, 51–60, 2005.
3. Fard, N. S. and Gunawan, I., Reliability Bounds for Large Multistage Interconnection Networks, *Lecture Notes in Computer Science*, Vol. 2367, 507–514, 2002.
4. Gunawan, I. and Fard, N.S., Terminal Reliability Assessment of Gamma and Extra-Stage Gamma Networks, *International Journal of Quality and Reliability Management*, Vol. 29, No. 7, 820–831, 2012.
5. Gunawan, I. and Gan, M. L., Reliability Analysis of Gamma Interconnection Network Systems, *International Journal of Performability* Engineering, Vol. 5, No. 5, 485–492, 2009.
6. Gunawan, I., Redundant Paths and Reliability Bounds in Gamma Networks, *Applied Mathematical Modelling*, Vol. 32, No. 4, 588–594, 2008.

10

Terminal Reliability Assessment of Gamma and Extra-Stage Gamma Networks

10.1   Introduction

A major challenge in designing large-scale parallel/distributed systems is the construction of an interconnection network to provide inter-processor communication and in some cases, memory access for the processors [6]. High frequency and large amounts of data transmission are major factors for designing interconnection network systems. Interconnection networks provide communication among processors, memory modules, and other devices in parallel computer systems. Among several advantages of multistage interconnection networks are: high reliability through backup and redundancy, high speed in data transmission, maximum performance through interconnection among processors, and low cost [5, 15, 18]. This paper presents a methodology for the reliability evaluation of a specific structure of MINs, known as gamma and extra-stage gamma networks.

MINs connect input devices to output devices through a number of switching stages in which each switch is a crossbar network. The properties of MINs can be broadly divided into three categories: 1-path MINs (non-redundant),

2-path MINs, and multi-path MINs (redundant) [2–4, 9–10]. A multi-path MIN is composed of switching elements (SEs) with at least 3 inputs and 3 outputs. The multiple path MINs provide multiple paths between each input-output pair of the network. Gamma and extra-stage gamma networks belong to this category [7, 14, 16].

In general, a single-path MIN only has a single path from a particular processor to a particular set of memories. A multi-path MIN consists of switches that have multi inputs and multi outputs. Therefore, the cost of hardware is higher for a multi-path MIN than that of a unique-path MIN in terms of number of stages, number of switches per stage, and the size of the switching elements. These are some of the principal factors that contribute to the switch complexity of a MIN. However, the multiple path systems have higher flexibility of data transmission. The major consideration in the design of the network is keeping the switch and link complexity as low as possible [1, 12–13, 17, 19].

Terminal Reliability, generally used as a measure of robustness of a MIN, is the probability of the existence of at least one fault free path between a designated pair of input (s) and output (t) terminals (two terminal) [9, 20]. This is denoted by R_{st} (G), where G is the network representing the system. A network G can be directed or undirected. In a directed network, there is at least one directed path between s and t. Different reliability measures and performance analyses of MINs have been studied in recent years [8, 11–12]. The terminal reliability of MINs can be defined as the probability that at least one path exists from a particular processor to a particular set of memories.

The following assumptions are commonly made for the terminal reliability evaluation of MINs [2]:

1. All failures are statistically independent.
2. All switching elements (SEs) are substantially less reliable than the links
3. Each SE in the MIN has two states: failure, or operational with a known reliability.
4. All SEs are identical and have constant exponential failure rates.
5. The SEs are not repairable. Source and terminal switches are always in operating condition.
6. A SE is in a failure state when it cannot perform any of the connection functions.

The next section presents Gamma network structure with an example demonstrating the routing pattern.

10.2   Gamma Network

A Gamma network is an interconnection network connecting N input switches to N output switches [7, 16]. It consists of $(\log_2 N) + 1$ stages with N switches per stage. In all but the first and last stages, each switching element consists of 3 input and 3 output switches. The switching elements of the first, or input stage, consist of 1 input and 3 outputs, and the last stage consists of 3 inputs and 1 output switches. The Gamma networks are structured in such a way to allow for redundant paths between the input and output switches, leading to a high fault tolerance.

Reliability evaluation of large-scale Gamma networks could be really tedious, since there could be many alternative routes connecting two specific switching elements (source and terminal). In this paper, a method for identifying different routes from each source to each destination based on routing tags is discussed. Then, the corresponding terminal reliability can be evaluated according to routes leading to a specific destination.

10.2.1   Routing Pattern in Gamma Network

Information originating from a source can change its route at intermediate stages before reaching its destination. There are three possible interconnections from stage i to stage i + 1: the data from SE j at stage i $[0 \le i \le (\log_2 N)$ and $0 \le j \le N - 1]$ can take the straight path to output cell j, or take the upward path to reach cell $(j - 2^i) \bmod N$, or take the downward path to reach cell $(j + 2^i) \bmod N$. The expression u mod v is the remainder of u divided by v (i.e., $(7 + 2^i) \bmod 8$ is 1).

For a given source s and a given destination t, where s and t lie in the range of 0 to N − 1, the tag value δ is defined as $\delta = |t - s|$, where $0 \le \delta \le N - 1$. Then, the number of redundant paths for each tag value in the network can be determined. The reliability of all redundant paths for a given tag value is the same. That is, for a given tag value, there are $P_n(\delta)$ redundant paths available in the system.

It is interesting to observe that except for tag value 0, there are always multiple representations for routing tags. This means that for a source-s and destination-t pair, there is only one path if s = t, and more than one path if s ≠ t.

In a Gamma network, any switching element at the intermediate stages consists of 3 incoming and 3 outgoing links. A routing tag is used to guide the information through the network. In this network, the routing tag consists of (n − 1) digits. Each digit in the routing tag will be either 1, 0, or −1. In the routing tag of SE j at stage i, the 1, 0, and −1 digits indicate that the input is from switching element k of stage (i – 1) where (k < j), (k = j), and (k > j) respectively. In other words, at the stage i, SE j can receive inputs from three SEs: j, $(j - 2^{i-1})$ mod N, $(j + 2^{i-1})$ mod N of stage (i – 1). These three inputs will respectively have 0, 1, and (-1) in the mth digit of their tags. The three inputs can be routed to three different SEs if the mth digits of their tags are all different. However, if any two of the inputs have the same m^{th} digit in their tags, then there is a conflict. Such a conflict can be avoided, in most cases, by using alternate forms of the tags, except when a tag value is 0. Therefore, there is a considerable flexibility in selecting routes for permuting data in this network.

In this section, the distribution of paths for various tag values is discussed. It is considered that the network consists of $N = 2^{n-1}$ input and N output switching elements. As the tags consist of n digits, the total number of paths is 3^{n-1}. The tag values lie in the range of $-(N - 1)$ to $+(N - 1)$. It can be observed that a tag value +i and (i – N) are equivalent, as they route data to the same destination from a particular source. Also, when source s > N-1, the routing process from s is equivalent to s – N and when the destination t > N – 1, the routing pattern to t is equivalent to t – N. Hence, only the routing process for positive values are considered as distinct tags, and the negative tags will be treated as alternate forms for some positive tags.

10.2.2   Redundant Paths

Now consider the Gamma network of Figure 10.1, for the flow of data from source 2 to destination 5, and N is 8. The tag value of this connection is |5–2|=3 mod 8, which is equal to 3. The binary redundant forms for the tag value of 3 are (1,-1,1), (1,-1,-1), (-1,0,1), (-1,0,-1) and (1,1,0). Also for source 5 and destination 2, the tag value is |2–5| mod 8 also is equal to 3, which can be represented as (-1,1,1), (-1,1,-1), (1,0,-1), (1,0,1), and (-1,-1,0). Therefore, for a tag value of 3, there are 5 redundant paths, identified by the three digits of routing tags. Interestingly, except for the tag value of 0, there are always multiple representations for routing tags. This means that for a source s and destination t pair, there is only one path if s = t and more than one path if s ≠ t. All redundant representations for tag values of 3 are valid routing tags for routing data from source 2 to destination 5 and from source 5 to destination 2. It should be noted that the first digit of the routing tags is the most significant, since it determines the routing paths in the network. Notice that in the example above, the first digit of routing tags from source 2 to destination 5 is the opposite sign of the first digit of routing tags from source 5 to destination 2.

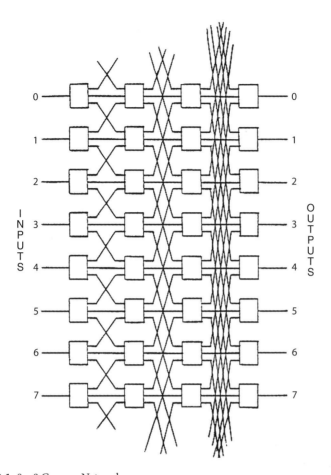

Figure 10.1 8 x 8 Gamma Network.

Now the number of paths for different tags can be calculated. The distribution of paths for various tags with increasing orders of N are presented in Table 10.1.

The number of paths for various tags can be calculated by the following formula [16]:

$$
P_n(x) = \begin{cases} P_{n-1}(\dfrac{x}{2}) & \text{if x is even} \\[2em] P_{n-1}(\dfrac{x-1}{2}) + P_{n-1}(\dfrac{x+1}{2}) & \text{if x is odd} \end{cases}
$$

The maximum value of $P_n(x)$ for a gamma network of size N follows the Fibonacci series $\{F_n\}$ (the n-th value is the summation of the two previous values) with increasing n.

Table 10.1 Number of Paths Associated with Tag values, n, and N.

N	2	4	8	16
n	2	3	4	5
Tag value (δ)	Number of paths			
0	1	1	1	1
1	2	3	4	5
2		2	3	4
3		3	5	7
4			2	3
5			5	8
6			3	5
7			4	7
8				2
9				7
10				5
11				8
12				3
13				7
14				4
15				5
Total	3	9	27	81

The maximum value of P_n (d) for a Gamma network of size N follows the Fibonacci series, where $P_n = P_{n-1} + P_{n-2}$ with increasing n:
2, 3, 5, 8, 13, 21, ...   for n = 2, 3, 4, 5, 6, ... where $P_0 = 1$, $P_1 = 1$.

The maximum number of paths is thus the n-th term of the series
1 2 3 5 8 13 21 ...   for n = 1, 2, ...

The minimum number of paths is of course equal to 1, so that P_n (0) = 1 for all n.

10.3   Terminal Reliability of Gamma Network

The terminal reliability of the 8 x 8-gamma network for different tag values computed by generating all possible paths between each source and destination pair of the network of Figure 10.1 is summarized in Table 10.2.

Expressions for terminal reliability evaluation of each tag value are developed based on network reliability methods, such as path method, cut set method, or conditional probability procedure [8, 11]. For a tag value of 2, there are 3 paths connecting 4 switching elements of four stages as shown in Figure 10.2. The single switch at stage "0" is connected in series to a single switch at stage "1", and they are in series with the two parallel switching elements at stage 2, and this is connected in series to a single switch at terminal stage 3. Therefore the reliability expression for tag value 2 is $r^2 (1-(1-r)^2)r = 2r^4 - r^5$.

Table 10.2 Terminal Reliability of 8X8 Gamma Networks a Function r and δ.

Tag value (δ)	Number of paths	Terminal Reliability
0	1	r^4
1	4	$3r^4 - 3r^5 + r^6$
2	3	$2r^4 - r^5$
3	5	$3r^4 - 3r^5 + r^6$
4	2	r^4
5	5	$3r^4 - 3r^5 + r^6$
6	3	$2r^4 - r^5$
7	4	$3r^4 - 3r^5 + r^6$

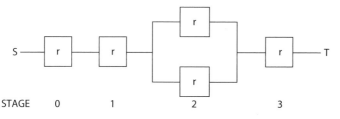

Figure 10.2 Reliability Block Diagram for Tag Value 2.

Likewise, the reliability expression for tag value 3, using path method is: $r^2 (3r^2 -3r^3 + r^4)= 3r^4 - 3r^5 + r^6$, where the first r^2 represents the source and terminal reliability and the remaining term is the reliability of stages one and two in series as illustrated in Figure 10.3.

Table 10.3 presents the evaluation of terminal reliability of the 8 x 8-gamma network for various tags, as a function of the reliability of a switching element. The terminal reliability is calculated by conditioning a stage and proceeding through all possible combinations of the network and assuming that the switching element at the input and output stage work for the system to be operational. It can be observed from the table that as the number of possible paths increases for different values of tags, the terminal reliability also increases. The terminal reliability graph for the tag value 0, 1, and 2 is illustrated in Figure 10.4 accordingly.

10.4   Extra-Stage Gamma Network

Gamma network is based on the $(+/-)2^i$ connection patterns. In such a network there exist multiple paths to connect a source s to a destination t, except when s = t. The number of paths for (s, t) is a function of the tag value (t - s) modulo N, and the size of the network N [14].

An extra-stage gamma network is constructed by adding an extra stage to the original gamma network as illustrated in Figure 10.5. Multiple paths are provided for all the tag values including 0. The extra stage can be any stage out of n = $\log_2 N$ stages of the original network. The extra stage of 0, 1, -1 connection patterns gives the most uniform distribution, and also results in a 1-fault tolerant interconnection network.

Figure 10.5 also shows that there are 9 possible paths for s = 3 and t = 3 connection pair. This is one of the advantages of the extra-stage gamma

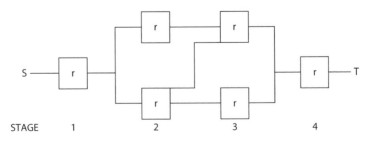

Figure 10.3 Reliability Block Diagram for Tag Value 3.

Table 10.3 Terminal Reliability Evaluation of the 8 x 8 Gamma Network.

SE	Terminal Reliability of the Gamma Network for the Tag Value δ							
Reliability	**0**	**1**	**2**	**3**	**4**	**5**	**6**	**7**
0.99	0.9606	0.9703	0.9702	0.9703	0.9606	0.9703	0.9702	0.9703
0.98	0.9224	0.9412	0.9408	0.9412	0.9224	0.9412	0.9408	0.9412
0.96	0.8493	0.8847	0.8833	0.8847	0.8493	0.8847	0.8833	0.8847
0.95	0.8145	0.8573	0.8552	0.8573	0.8145	0.8573	0.8552	0.8573
0.94	0.7807	0.8304	0.8276	0.8304	0.7807	0.8304	0.8276	0.8304
0.92	0.7164	0.7783	0.7737	0.7783	0.7164	0.7783	0.7737	0.7783
0.90	0.6561	0.7283	0.7217	0.7283	0.6561	0.7283	0.7217	0.7283

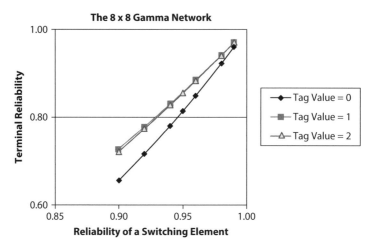

Figure 10.4 Terminal Reliability Graph of the 8 x 8 Gamma Network.

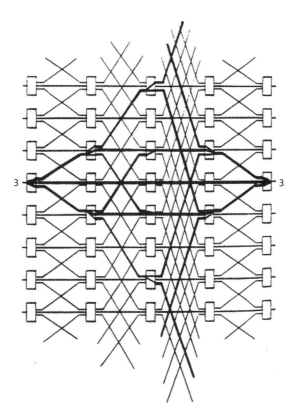

Figure 10.5 8 x 8 Extra-Stage Gamma Network with. 9 Paths Between (s=3, t=3) Pair Connection.

network compared to the original gamma network, that has only a single path when s = t. The numbers of paths for different tags in the extra-stage gamma network are presented in Table 10.4.

The computation of terminal reliability of the 8 x 8 extra-stage gamma network for various tags, as a function of the reliability of a switching element is shown in Table 10.5. Let q be the probability of a faulty switch. The terminal reliability evaluation of the 8 x 8 extra-stage gamma network for different tag values are presented in Table 10.6 respectively.

Table 10.4 Number of Paths Associated with Tag value, n, and N in Extra-Stage Gamma Network.

N	2	4	8	16
n	3	4	5	6
Tag value (δ)	Number of paths			
0	5	7	9	11
1	4	6	8	10
2		8	12	16
3		6	10	14
4			12	18
5			10	16
6			12	20
7			8	14
8				16
9				14
10				20
11				16
12				18
13				14
14				16
15				10
Total	9	27	81	243

Table 10.5 Terminal Reliability of 8X8 Extra-Stage Gamma Network as a Function of r and δ.

Tag value (δ)	# of paths	Terminal Reliability
0	9	$r^{13}+7r^{12}q+(33r^{11}+r^5)q^2+(104r^{10}+8r^8)q^3+(190r^9+31r^7)q^4+(160r^8+26r^6)q^5+(60r^7+6r^5)q^6+8r^6q^7$
1	8	$r^{13}+(5r^{12}+r^{10}+r^7)q+(23r^{11}+2r^9+3r^6+r^5)q^2+(73r^{10}+6r^8+r^6+2r^5)q^3+(129r^9+20r^7+3r^5)q^4+(99r^8+13r^6)q^5+26r^7q^6$
2	12	$r^{14}+(6r^{13}+r^{11})q+(30r^{12}+4r^{10}+2r^9+r^6)q^2+(108r^{11}+14r^9+6r^8+2r^7+2r^6+2r^5)q^3+(231r^{10}+23r^8+10r^7+4r^6+6r^5)q^4+(280r^9+28r^7+4r^6)q^5+(160r^8+10r^6)q^6+32r^7q^7$
3	10	$r^{13}+(5r^{12}+r^{10}+r^7)q+(23r^{11}+2r^9+3r^6+r^5)q^2+(73r^{10}+6r^8+r^6+2r^5)q^3+(129r^9+20r^7+3r^5)q^4+(99r^8+13r^6)q^5+26r^7q^6$
4	12	$r^{13}+7r^{12}q+(33r^{11}+r^5)q^2+(104r^{10}+8r^8)q^3+(190r^9+31r^7)q^4+(160r^8+26r^6)q^5+(60r^7+6r^5)q^6+8r^6q^7$
5	10	$r^{13}+(5r^{12}+r^{10}+r^7)q+(23r^{11}+2r^9+3r^6+r^5)q^2+(73r^{10}+6r^8+r^6+2r^5)q^3+(129r^9+20r^7+3r^5)q^4+(99r^8+13r^6)q^5+26r^7q^6$
6	12	$r^{14}+(6r^{13}+r^{11})q+(30r^{12}+4r^{10}+2r^9+r^6)q^2+(108r^{11}+14r^9+6r^8+2r^7+2r^6+2r^5)q^3+231r^{10}+23r^8+10r^7+4r^6+6r^5)q^3+(280r^9+28r^7+4r^6)q^5+(160r^8+10r^6)q^6+32r^7q^7$
7	8	$r^{13}+(5r^{12}+r^{10}+r^7)q+(23r^{11}+2r^9+3r^6+r^5)q^2+(73r^{10}+6r^8+r^6+2r^5)q^3+(129r^9+20r^7+3r^5)q^4+(99r^8+13r^6)q^5+26r^7q^6$

Table 10.6 Terminal Reliability Evaluation of the 8 x 8 Extra-Stage Gamma Network.

SE Reliability	Terminal Reliability of the Extra-Stage Gamma Network for the Tag Value δ							
	0	1	2	3	4	5	6	7
0.99	0.9427	0.9429	0.9338	0.9429	0.9427	0.9429	0.9338	0.9429
0.98	0.8906	0.8912	0.8746	0.8912	0.8906	0.8912	0.8746	0.8912
0.96	0.8000	0.8020	0.7746	0.8020	0.8000	0.8020	0.7746	0.8020
0.95	0.7607	0.7635	0.7326	0.7635	0.7607	0.7635	0.7326	0.7635
0.94	0.7250	0.7285	0.6951	0.7285	0.7250	0.7285	0.6951	0.7285
0.92	0.6627	0.6675	0.6317	0.6675	0.6627	0.6675	0.6317	0.6675
0.90	0.6108	0.6163	0.5809	0.6163	0.6108	0.6163	0.5809	0.6163

In general, it can be seen from the Table 10.6 that the terminal reliability of the extra-stage gamma network is much lower than that of the gamma network. In this case, the extra-stage provides more possible paths for each tag value, and hence leads to more switching elements subject to failure. It can be observed that the number of possible paths of the extra-stage gamma network for the tag value 0 is 9, compared to that of the gamma network that only has one path. The terminal reliability graph for the tag value 0, 1, and 2 is illustrated in Figure 10.6.

10.5 Comparison

A comparison between terminal reliability of the gamma network and the extra-stage gamma network, as a function of the reliability of a switching element for the 8 x 8 case using the tag value 0, is shown in Figure 10.7. It can be observed that the terminal reliability of the 8 x 8 extra-stage gamma network is lower than that of the 8 x 8 gamma network, and the difference between the terminal reliability of both networks reduces as the reliability of switching elements increases.

10.6 Conclusions

In this paper, terminal reliability as a function of the reliability of a switching element of MINs is analyzed. Terminal Reliability, generally used as a measure of robustness of a MIN, is the probability of existence of at least one fault

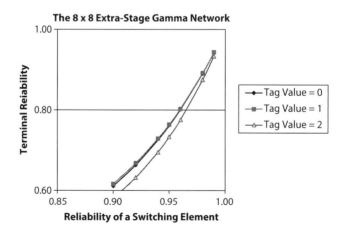

Figure 10.6 Terminal Reliability Graph of the 8 x 8 Extra-Stage Gamma Network.

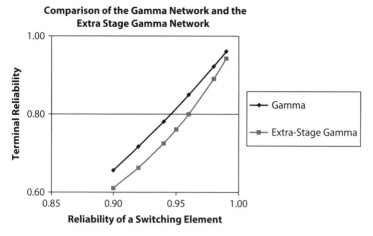

Figure 10.7 Comparison of Terminal Reliability Graph of the Gamma Network and the Extra-Stage Gamma Network for the 8 x 8 Case using Tag Value 0.

free path between a designated pair of input (s) and output (t) terminals. The fault-tolerance and terminal reliability capabilities as well as the reliability of these networks are evaluated. It is observed that the additional stage provides more redundant paths in the networks. Therefore, an additional stage leads to extra paths and improves the system's fault tolerance. It has been shown that in a Shuffle-Exchange Network Systems, an addition of an extra stage leads to higher terminal reliability of that network [9]. However, the additional stage does not necessarily improve the terminal reliability of the gamma network. The additional stage could add to the switch complexity and increase the probability of a path failure as well. Therefore, the extra-stage gamma network has multiple paths in every source-destination pair including the case when the tag value is 0, that is, when (s = t).

References

1. Arzilawati N., Yunus, Md. and Othman, M., Shuffle Exchange Network in Multistage Interconnection Network: A Review and Challenges, *International Journal of Computer and Electrical Engineering*, Vol. 3, No. 5, 724–728, 2011.
2. Blake, J. T. and K. S. Trivedi, Multistage Interconnection Network Reliability, *IEEE Transactions on Computers*, 38 (11), (1989), 1600–1604.
3. Blake, J. T. and K. S Trivedi, Reliability Analysis of Interconnection Networks Using Hierarchical Composition, *IEEE Transactions on Reliability*, 38 (1), (1989), 111–119.
4. Booting, C., S. Rai, and D.P. Agrawal, Reliability Computation of Multistage Interconnection Networks, *IEEE Transactions on Reliability*, 38 (1), (1989), 138–145.

5. Choi, M., N. Park N., F. J. Meyer, and F. Lombardi, Performance Analysis of Fault Tolerance Multistage Interconnection Networked Parallel Instrumentation with Concurrent Testing and Diagnosis, *IEEE Instrumentation and Measurement Technology Conference*, Anchorage, USA, (2002), 21–23.

6. Duato, J., S. Yalmanchili, and L. M. Ni, *Interconnection Networks an Engineering Approach*, CA: IEEE Computer Society, (1997).

7. El Sayed, Y., Venkatesan, R., and Sivakumar, H., "Fault Tolerance and Reliability Analyses of the Balanced Gamma Network," *International Journal of Parallel and Distributed Systems and Networks*, 2 (4), (1999), 244–254.

8. Fard, N. S. and T.H. Lee, Spanning Tree Approach in All Terminal Network Reliability Expansion, Computer Communication Journal, 24 (13), (2001), 1348–1353.

9. Fard, N. S. and I. Gunawan, Terminal Reliability Improvement of Shuffle-Exchange Network Systems, International Journal of Reliability, Quality, and Safety Engineering, 12 (1), (2005), 01-10.

10. Gunawan, I., "Reliability Analysis of Shuffle-Exchange Network Systems", *Reliability Engineering and System Safety*, Vol. 93, No. 2, 271-276, 2008.

11. Gunawan, I., "Performance Analysis of a Multistage Interconnection Network System Based on a Minimum Cut Set Method", *International Journal of Performability Engineering*, Vol. 4, No. 2, 111–120, 2008.

12. Gunawan, I., "Multistage Interconnection Networks Reliability Evaluation Based on Stratified Sampling Monte Carlo Method", *International Journal of Modelling and Simulation*, Vol. 28, No. 2, 209–214, 2008.

13. Kamiura, N., T. Kodera, and N. Matsui, Design of a Fault Tolerant Multistage Interconnection Network with Parallel Duplicated Switches, *IEEE International Workshop on Defect and Fault Tolerance in VLSI Systems*, (2000), 143–151.

14. Lee, K. Y. and W. Hegazy, The Extra Stage Gamma Network, *Computer*, (1986), 175–182.

15. McMillen, R. J., A Survey of Interconnection Networks, *Proceeding of Globecom*, (1984), 105–113.

16. Parker, D. S. and C. S.Raghavendra, The Gamma Network, *IEEE Transactions on Computers*, 33 (4), (1984), 367–373.

17. Raghavendra, C. and A. Varma, Reliability Analysis of Redundant-Path Interconnection Networks, *IEEE Transactions on Reliability*, 38, (1), (1989), 130–137.

18. Sengupta, J. P. K. Bansal , High Speed Dynamic Fault-Tolerance, *IEEE Region 10 International Conference on Electrical and Electronic Technology*, (2001), 669–675.

19. Sharma, S., Bansal, P.K. and Kahlon, K.S., On a Class of Multistage Interconnection Network in Parallel Processing, *International Journal of Computer Science and Network Security*, Vol. 8, No. 5, 287–291, 2008.

20. Yeh Fu-Min, Lu Shyue-Kung, and Kuo Sy-Yen, OBDD – Based Evaluation of k – Terminal Network Reliability, 51(4), (2002), 443–451.

11

Reliability Prediction of Distributed Systems Using Monte Carlo Method

11.1 Introduction

The demand for even more computing power has never stopped. A number of important problems have been identified in the areas of defense, aerospace, automotive applications, weather forecasting, map making, aerodynamic simulations, chemical reaction simulations, seismic data processing, air traffic control, robot vision, and science, whose solution requires tremendous amount of computational power. There are fundamental considerations as speed of computer device reaches a limit and an execution rate required simply beyond the capabilities of current large computer systems. Hence, these facts result that the system performance in the future can only significantly increased through additional concurrent processing. As a result, parallel computers with multiple processors can supply the support essential to meeting the computational performance goals for all these applications. The means for communication among processors, memory modules, and other devices of a parallel computer is the interconnection network.

Interconnection networks are a natural result of advances in computer technology that provide the need in the improved system performance. As computer systems evolved, the hardware costs being a significant limiting factor. However, interconnection technology is creating an entirely new atmosphere; it is now economically feasible to construct a multiple-processor computer system by interconnecting a large number of processors and memory modules. Interconnection networks are currently being used for many different applications such as telephone switches, processor/memory interconnects for supercomputer, networks for industrial application, and wide area computer networks. Therefore, concept, design, and implementation of interconnection networks are crucial factors at this point in time.

Multistage Interconnection Network (MIN) falls within the category of indirect network. It has been used in both circuit switching and packet switching networks with the introduction of buffered switches. These include multiprocessor and communication network environments such as Ultracomputer [1], NEC Cenju-3, Cenju-4 [12], IBM RP3, ATM switches [16], Gigabit Ethernet [5] and optical network [19]. The number of stages, interconnection design and the type of switching element (SE) used in the network configuration differentiate each MIN, for example shuffle exchange network, gamma network [3], extra stage gamma network [11], delta network, Tandem-Banyan network [16] and multilayer MIN [7].

The variety and the extensive usage MIN prompt for a method that could provide efficient evaluation of various MIN reliabilities in order to select the best MIN topology. Various methods have been used to evaluate the reliability of a network such as neural network [6], derivation of bounds [2, 8] and sum of disjoint product [14]. This paper presents a method to estimate the reliability of MIN based on Monte Carlo method as the exact reliability calculation for larger networks are very complex.

A single type of MIN, known as shuffle exchange network with an additional stage (SEN+) that is specifically for multiprocessor environment is discussed. The layout of the MIN topology is shown in Fig. 11.1 with number of inputs, N = 8. The rectangles in the figure represent the 2x2 switching elements (SEs) which provide the interconnection between inputs and outputs. The SE can either transmit the inputs straight or has crossed connections. Hence, a working SE can be in any of the four connection patterns as shown in Fig. 11.2. The SEN+ system has N inputs and N outputs. There are two paths between each source-destination pair. It has n = ($\log_2$ N) + 1 stages and each stage has N/2 switching elements. In general, the switch complexity for the N x N SEN+ is N/2 ($\log_2$ N + 1). Thus, the additional cost of the SEN+ is N/2 switches or a fractional increase of 1/$\log_2$ N, is small for a large N.

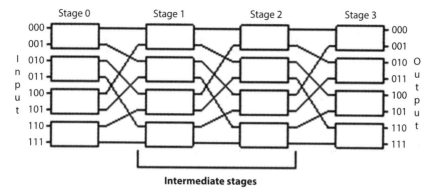

Figure 11.1 8x8 SEN+ topology.

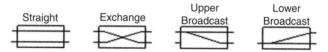

Figure 11.2 Connection pattern for 2x2 SE.

The control strategy allows a switching element in stage 0 to use the T (straight) setting until a failure in a SE along the path from a given S to a given D is detected. At that time, the SE in stage 0 is placed in the X (exchange) setting for all future accesses between that S-D pair. In this way, it is shown that two paths between each S-D pair given that the failures occur only in the intermediate stages of the SEN+. It is recognized that in actual implementations, the network should be reconfigured to reduce congestion.

SEN+ is a hybrid of generic shuffle exchange network (SEN) with higher failure tolerance than SEN. It has two disjoint redundant paths in the intermediate stages thus able to tolerate a single path failure.

The problem of determining the reliability of a complex system, whose components are subject to failure, has received considerable attention in the statistical, engineering, and operations research literature. Indeed, in certain situations, improving the reliability of a system can be more consequential than reducing its cost. Reliability analysis can be applied to a variety of practical systems, ranging from large-scale telecommunication, transportation, and mechanical systems, to the microelectronic scale of integrated circuits.

Network reliability is commonly arises from the interconnection of various elements in the form of a network or a graph. For example, the nodes of a multistage interconnection network might represent the physical locations of switching elements and its edges might represent existing communication links between switching elements. In realistic settings, the elements of a network, its nodes or edges or both, are subject to failure, but in most analysis only the links are considered as failing components. At any stage, each element is either working or failed; as a result, the network itself is also either working or failed. In the multi-stage interconnection networks example, working might mean that a distinguished input switching element and distinguished output switching element are able to communicate over operational links of the network, while failure means that there is no complete transmission path in the system.

In the next sections, reliability parameters (terminal, broadcast, and network reliability) are discussed, Monte Carlo method and algorithm to calculate the point estimate and bound reliability are presented, numerical results are shown to prove the applicability of the proposed method with the exact reliability.

11.2 Reliability Parameters

Reliability of the network is concerned with the ability of a network to carry out its desired network operation successfully. In our case, interconnection networks for processor-processor and processor-memory information exchanges in multiprocessing parallel processing systems, contribute appreciably to the performance as well as the reliability of the overall system. The reliability measures of particular interest are: terminal reliability (TR), broadcast reliability (BR), and network reliability (NR).

1. *Terminal Reliability* (TR). Terminal reliability, generally used as a measure of robustness of a MIN, is the probability of existence of at least one fault free path between a designated pair of input and output terminals (two terminals).
2. *Broadcast Reliability* (BR). Another useful measure of the reliability of a MIN is its ability to broadcast data from a given input terminal to all the output terminals of the network. A network is said to have failed when a connection cannot be made from the given input terminal to at least one of the output terminals.
3. *Network Reliability* (NR). The network reliability is defined as the probability that there exists a connection between each input to all outputs (all terminals).

Exact reliability of SEN+ can be determined by evaluating all possible SE states but it is NP-hard due to the huge possibilities of SE states as the number of inputs increases. Monte Carlo method is able to provide a point estimate of SEN+ reliability without evaluating every possible SE state. It is based on the adaptation of a method proposed by Fishman [15]. Monte Carlo (MC) method enables estimation of SEN+ reliability via random sampling of SE states.

11.3   Monte Carlo Method

Monte Carlo method provides estimation based on sampling random-ization. Results generated from crude Monte Carlo method might not be accurate. In this section, the benefit accrued from applying stratified sampling is explored. Crude Monte Carlo method (without any variance reduction) is based on random sampling of SEs's states and then is evalu-ated for its connectivity. This process is repeated for a specific number of times as defined by n_r. It does not require any partitioning as it being done in stratified sampling. Crude Monte Carlo method has an inherent weak-ness which is the sampling performed may be weighted to certain number of working SE samples, which may cause the result to be imprecise [15].

The following assumptions are defined to facilitate the estimation of SEN+ reliability:

   i.   A SE can only have two states; working = 1 or failed = 0.
   ii. All SE failures are statistically independent and random. A SE is assumed failed when it could not be in any of the four connection patterns; lower broadcast, upper broadcast, straight or exchange pattern (Fig. 11.2).
   iii. SE is assumed to be less reliable than the link and cannot be repaired.
   iv. All SEs have identical reliability.
   v.   All SEs in the first and last stages are assumed to be working.

Algorithm 1: Monte Carlo Method (MC) for SEN+

Parameters:

1. Number of SEs in the intermediate stages, n_{im}
2. SE reliability, r(t)
3. Number of inputs, N

4. Number of replications, n_r
5. Number of SE in the first and last stages, n_{fl}.
6. Reliability of SEN+, R

Procedure:

1. SET accumulated reliability, $R_{ac} = 0$
   SET number of working switches, $n_{working} = 1$
   SET number of SE in intermediate stages, n_{im}
   SET total number of samplings, $n_{sampled} = 0$
   SET total connected network, $n_{connected} = 0$

2. REPEAT
   Note: Calculate the stratum sampling size for each stratum. Number of stratum depends on the number of working SEs in the intermediate stages.
   SET number of sampling for stratum i $(i = n_{working})$,

   $$n_{stratum\_size} = n_r \cdot \left(\frac{n_{im}}{n_{working}} \right) \cdot r(t)^{n_{im}} \cdot [1 - r(t)]^{n_{working}}$$

   SET $n_{sampled} = n_{sampled} + n_{stratum\_size}$
   Note: Evaluate only when the number of working SEs in the intermediate stages is at least half of the total number of the SEs in the intermediate stages. The SEN+ fails when the number of working SEs in the intermediate stages is less than half of its total.
       IF $n_{working} \geq n_{im} \times 0.5$ THEN
   Note: The interconnection still functions even there is a single SE failure. Evaluation is skipped as the interconnection is functioning when there is only a single SE failure.
   IF $n_{working} < n_{im} - 1$ THEN
   Note: Generated SE states are dependent on the type of interconnection; terminal, broadcast or network.
   Randomly generate SE states in intermediate stages in array state$[n_{im}]$
   Note: Evaluation of SEN+ network is dependent on the type of interconnection; terminal, broadcast or network. This is done by evaluating the array state$[n_{im}]$.
   IF the SEN+ network is connected THEN
       $n_{connected} = n_{connected} + 1$
   END IF
   ELSE
       $n_{connected} = n_{connected} + n_{stratum\_size}$

END IF

$$n_{working} = n_{working} + 1$$
$$\text{UNTIL } (n_{working} \leq n_{im})$$

3. The estimated reliability for intermediate stages is multiplied with all the SE reliability for first and last stages to calculate the overall estimated reliability.

$$\text{RETURN } R = (n_{connected} / n_{sampled}) \cdot r(t)^{n}{}_{fl}$$

Algorithm 1 shows the procedure to perform Monte Carlo method with stratified sampling. Stratified sampling allows us to achieve better approximation of the exact SEN+ reliability. It partitions the sample into several stratums, where each stratum contains homogenous elements. This allows sampling to be performed on important stratums and ignores irrelevant ones, thus improving the accuracy and efficiency of the estimation. Stratum sampling size is based on proportional allocation derived from binomial probability distribution which is defined as

$$n_{stratum\_size} = n_r \left(\frac{n_{im}}{n_{working}} \right) r(t)^{n}{}_{im} [1 - r(t)]^{n}{}_{working}$$

11.4   Confidence Interval for Monte Carlo Point Estimate

Confidence interval (Upper Limit, UL and Lower Limit, LL) of the point estimate reliability value using Monte Carlo method is derived using statistical non-parametric bootstrapping method [4, 10]. Non-parametric bootstrapping does not require any assumptions being made on the distribution pattern thus removing any errors that may result biased outcome. The bootstrapping method used to estimate the confidence interval in this paper is based on Efron's percentile confidence limit.

Efron's percentile confidence limit is used to determine confidence interval via bootstrapping. Figure 11.3–11.5 shows the box-plots for 100, 1000, 3000 and 10000 replications with 3000 bootstrap samples for SE reliability of 0.990990. It can be seen that for 100 replications, the distribution is slightly negative skewed. Lower whiskers of the box-plots can be seen to extend more than upper whiskers for 100 replications which indicates that the computed confidence interval is not reliable for small number of replications. The distribution is converging to symmetric distribution as the number of replications increase from 100 to 3000 replications as the upper

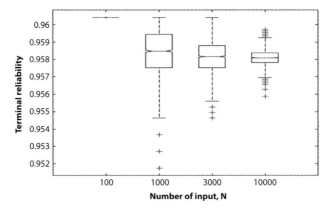

Figure 11.3 Bootstrap terminal reliability samples with 100, 1000, 3000 and 10000 replications for N = 128 with SE reliability = 0.990990.

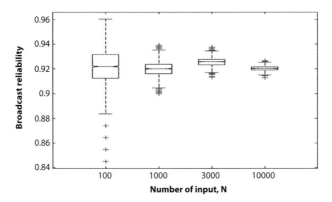

Figure 11.4 Bootstrap broadcast reliability samples with 100, 1000, 3000 and 10000 replications for N = 128 with SE reliability = 0.990990.

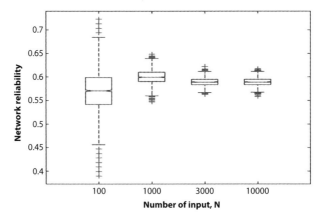

Figure 11.5 Bootstrap network reliability samples with 100, 1000, 3000 and 10000 replications for N = 128 with SE reliability = 0.990990.

and lower whickers balanced out each other. This verifies that confidence interval acquired from Efron's percentile confidence limit is only reliable with at least 1000 replications.

Similar settings for the box-plots with SE reliability of 0.990990 were used to generate histograms, as depicted in Figure11.6–11.8. It can be seen that the distributions are converging to bell-curved shape as the number of replication increases with. This means that simulation with larger samples size will likely to be distributed normally, thus producing a more reliable confidence interval. Based on this assertion, comparison made between Monte Carlo method and other methods in the later sections will be based on 6000 replications to ensure the results generated are reliable.

11.5   Numerical Results

We implemented several other methods on single software platform to gauge our level of accuracy by comparing the results. These include exact terminal reliability of SEN+ calculated using the mathematical (Math) approach [8, 17], Fard and Gunawan's method [13] to calculate exact broadcast and network reliabilities up to N = 16 inputs and Blake and Trivedi's network reliability bounds [9]. For higher number of inputs, we compare our results against Cheng and Ibe's results published in their paper [18]. For the MC

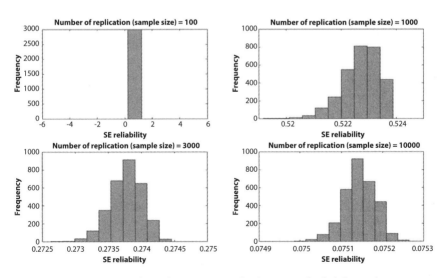

Figure 11.6 Histograms of 3000 bootstrap samples for terminal reliability with 100, 1000, 3000 and 10000 elements for N = 128 with SE reliability = 0.990990.

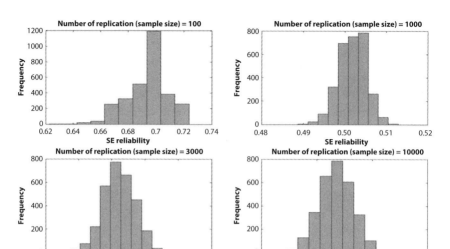

Figure 11.7 Histograms of 3000 bootstrap samples for broadcast reliability with 100, 1000, 3000 and 10000 elements for N = 128 with SE reliability = 0.990990.

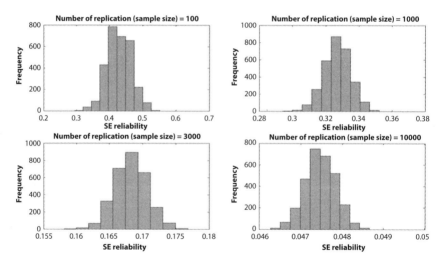

Figure 11.8 Histograms of 3000 bootstrap samples for network reliability with 100, 1000, 3000 and 10000 elements for N = 128 with SE reliability = 0.990990.

method we will use 6000 replications with 95% level of confidence based on 5000 bootstrap samples for the estimated point reliability value.

A measurement parameter to measure the accurateness of our method is used, known as the percentage of difference, α. It measures the difference between the Monte Carlo point estimate and the exact reliability value.

$$\alpha = \left| \frac{\text{Estimated value } - \text{ Exact value}}{\text{Exact value}} \right| \times 100\% \qquad (11.1)$$

Figure 11.9 shows that the confidence interval for Monte Carlo point estimate of terminal reliability envelopes all the exact values for N = 2048 inputs. Table 11.1 depicts the percentage of difference for terminal reliability is less than 0.024% for N = 16 inputs and 0.134% for N = 2048 inputs. Similar results are shown based on Monte Carlo point estimate for broadcast reliability. The confidence interval of Monte Carlo point estimate covers the exact reliability values for N = 1024 inputs, shown in Fig. 11.10. The percentage of difference for broadcast reliability as in Table 11.2 is less than 0.210% for N = 128 and 0.100% for N = 1024.

The Monte Carlo point estimate confidence interval for network reliability falls below Cheng and Ibe's lower bound are shown in Fig. 11.11. But it falls within the bounds of Blake and Trivedi's method. Nevertheless, Monte Carlo point estimate can be used as a source of network reliability estimation as the risk of overestimating the network reliability is lower compared to Cheng and Ibe's method. The percentage of difference for network reliability with N = 16 inputs is less than 0.084% as shown in Table 11.3.

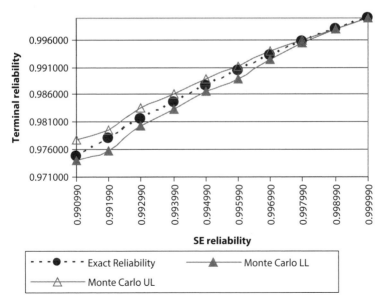

Figure 11.9 Exact value (Thanawastien & Gunawan's methods) and Monte Carlo point estimate of confidence interval of terminal reliability for N = 2048.

Table 11.1 Terminal reliability results for N = 16, 2048.

N	r(t)	Terminal Reliability				
		Math	Monte Carlo Method			α
		Exact	Point Estimate	LL	UL	
16	0.990990	0.981356	0.981406	0.980752	0.981898	0.0051
	0.991990	0.983485	0.983716	0.983224	0.984044	0.0235
	0.992990	0.985599	0.985700	0.985207	0.986029	0.0102
	0.993990	0.987699	0.987522	0.986863	0.988016	0.0179
	0.994990	0.989784	0.989675	0.989180	0.990005	0.0110
	0.995990	0.991854	0.991831	0.991500	0.991996	0.0023
	0.996990	0.993908	0.993823	0.993492	0.993989	0.0086
	0.997990	0.995948	0.995984	0.995984	0.995984	0.0036
	0.998990	0.997972	0.997981	0.997981	0.997981	0.0009
	0.999990	0.999980	0.999980	0.999980	0.999980	0.0000
2048	0.990990	0.974707	0.976005	0.974041	0.977806	0.1332
	0.991990	0.978168	0.977812	0.975844	0.979616	0.0364
	0.992990	0.981479	0.982085	0.980442	0.983564	0.0617
	0.993990	0.984635	0.984723	0.983241	0.986040	0.0089
	0.994990	0.987630	0.987860	0.986705	0.989015	0.0233
	0.995990	0.990457	0.990177	0.989020	0.991169	0.0283
	0.996990	0.993113	0.993161	0.992332	0.993823	0.0048
	0.997990	0.995589	0.995818	0.995486	0.995984	0.0230
	0.998990	0.997880	0.997981	0.997981	0.997981	0.0101
	0.999990	0.999980	0.999980	0.999980	0.999980	0.0000

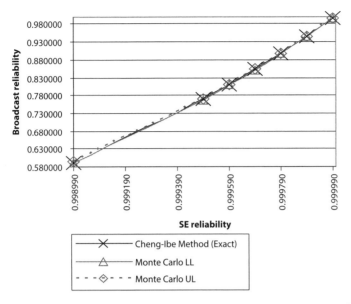

Figure 11.10 Exact value (Cheng-Ibe method) and Monte Carlo point estimate of confidence interval of broadcast reliability for N = 1024.

Table 11.2 Broadcast reliability results for N = 128, 1024.

N	r(t)	Cheng-Ibe Method	Monte Carlo Method			α
		Exact	Point Estimate	LL	UL	
128	0.990990	0.532779	0.531665	0.528796	0.534349	0.2091
	0.991990	0.573588	0.573420	0.570653	0.575990	0.0293
	0.992990	0.616968	0.616774	0.614137	0.619306	0.0314
	0.993990	0.663012	0.662531	0.660053	0.664896	0.0725
	0.994990	0.711806	0.711006	0.708721	0.713170	0.1124
	0.995990	0.763430	0.764500	0.762832	0.766168	0.1402
	0.996990	0.817951	0.818495	0.817125	0.819728	0.0665
	0.997990	0.875423	0.874923	0.873754	0.875947	0.0571
	0.998990	0.935883	0.936115	0.935647	0.936428	0.0248
	0.999990	0.999350	0.999350	0.999350	0.999350	0.0000

(Continued)

Table 11.2 (*Cont.*)

N	r(t)	Cheng-Ibe Method	Monte Carlo Method			α
		Exact	Point Estimate	LL	UL	
	0.998990	0.591132	0.591707	0.590417	0.592897	0.0973
	0.999490	0.768262	0.768718	0.767948	0.769360	0.0594
	0.999590	0.809266	0.809201	0.808391	0.809887	0.0080
1024	0.999690	0.852334	0.852097	0.851386	0.852665	0.0278
	0.999790	0.897560	0.897111	0.896363	0.897710	0.0500
	0.999890	0.945043	0.945130	0.945130	0.945130	0.0092
	0.999990	0.994882	0.994883	0.994883	0.994883	0.0001

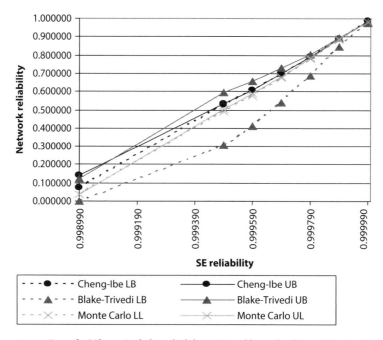

Figure 11.11 Bounds (Cheng & Ibe's and Blake & Trivedi's methods) and Monte Carlo point estimate of confidence interval of network reliability for N = 1024.

Table 11.3 Network reliability results for N = 16.

N	r(t)	Fard-Gunawan Method	Monte Carlo Method			α
		Actual	Point Estimate	LB	UB	
16	0.990990	0.860108	0.860425	0.858700	0.86201	0.0369
	0.991990	0.875158	0.875888	0.874420	0.87721	0.0834
	0.992990	0.890339	0.89057	0.889230	0.89176	0.0260
	0.993990	0.905644	0.905785	0.904570	0.90684	0.0155
	0.994990	0.921071	0.921091	0.920010	0.92201	0.0022
	0.995990	0.936613	0.936327	0.935390	0.93711	0.0305
	0.996990	0.952267	0.952594	0.952120	0.95291	0.0344
	0.997990	0.968026	0.967997	0.967510	0.96832	0.0030
	0.998990	0.983886	0.983798	0.983470	0.98396	0.0089
	0.999990	0.999840	0.999840	0.999840	0.99984	0.0000

11.6   Conclusion

In this paper, it is shown that Monte Carlo method with stratified sampling is capable of providing a good estimation on large shuffle-exchange network systems reliability. Low percentage of difference and the coverage of the confidence interval prove the applicability of Monte Carlo method.

As the Monte Carlo method is based on randomized sampling, results produced in each run may be different. Therefore, the mean of several runs can be used to have a better approximation value.

Some future work of the research would include the analysis of other type of MIN such as gamma network because the exact reliability of this network is difficult to get due to its complicated topology. Then, Monte Carlo method can be applied to resolve this difficulty.

References

1. A. Gottlied, *An overview of the NYU ultracomputer project*, Technical report (TR-086-U100), Department of Computer Science New York University, 1987.
2. A. Konak and A.E. Smith, *An improved general upperbound for all-terminal network reliability*, 1998, Retrieved August 14, 2003, from University of Pittsburgh Web site: http://www.pitt.edu/~aesmith/postscript/bound.pdf.
3. A. Vama and C.S. Raghavendra, "Performance analysis of redundant path interconnection networks", *Proceedings of International Conference of Parallel Processing*, pp. 474–479, 1985.
4. B. Efron and R. J. Tibshirani, *An introduction to the bootstrap*, Chapman and Hall, New York, 1993.
5. B. Y. Yu, *Analysis of a dual-receiver node with high fault tolerance for ultrafast OTDM packet switched shuffle networks*, Technical paper, 3COM, 1998.
6. C. Srivaree-ratana and A. E. Smith, "Estimation of all-terminal reliability using an artificial neural network", *Computers & Operations Research*, vol. 29, no. 7, pp. 849–868, 2002.
7. D. Tutsch and H. Gunter, "Multilayer multistage interconnection networks", *Proceedings of 2003 Design, Analysis, and Simulation of Distributed Systems (DASD'03)*, Orlando, USA, pp. 155–162, 2003.
8. Gunawan, I., "Reliability Analysis of Shuffle-Exchange Network Systems", *Reliability Engineering and System Safety*, Vol. 93, No. 2, 271–276, 2008.
9. J. Blake and K. S. Trivedi, "Multistage Interconnection Network Reliability", *IEEE Transactions on Computer*, vol. 38, no. 11, pp. 1600–1604, 1989.
10. J. Wang and R.J. Rao, "Weighted jackknife-after-bootstrap: a heuristic approach", *Proceedings of the 1997 Winter Simulation Conference*, pp. 240–245, 1997.
11. K.Y. Lee and W. Hegazy, "The extra stage gamma network", *IEEE Transactions on Computers*, vol. 37, no. 11, pp. 1445–1449, 1988.
12. NEC Corporation, *NEC releases highly parallel computer based on new memory architecture*, 1997, Retrieved August 14, 2003 from: http://www.nec.co.jp/press/en/9707/2801.html.
13. Fard, N. S. and Gunawan, I., "Terminal Reliability Improvement of Shuffle-Exchange Network Systems", *International Journal of Reliability, Quality and Safety Engineering*, Vol. 12, No. 1, 51–60, 2005.
14. P.J. Chua and C.L. Kuo, "A simple approach to the evaluation of multistage interconnection network reliability", *Proc. 37th Midwest Symp, Circuits and Systems*, pp. 313–316, 1994.
15. S. G. Fishman, *Monte Carlo: concepts, algorithms and applications*, Springer, New York, 1996.
16. S. Sibal and J. Zhang, "On a class of banyan networks and tandem banyan switching fabrics", *IEEE Transactions on Communications*, vol. 43, no.7, pp. 2231–2240, 1995.

17. S. Thanawastien, "The shuffle/exchange-plus networks", *Proceedings of the 20th annual Southeast regional conference*, pp. 89–96, 1982.

18. X. Cheng and O.C. Ibe, "Reliability of class of multistage interconnection networks", *IEEE Transactions on Parallel and Distributed Systems*, vol. 3, no. 2, pp. 241–246, 1992.

19. Y. Yang, "Permutation capability of optical multistage interconnection networks", *Journal of Parallel and Distributed Computing*, vol. 60, pp. 72–91, 2000.

Subject Index

Also of Interest

Check out these published and forthcoming titles in the Performability Engineering Series

Fundamentals of Reliability Engineering
By Indra Gunawan
Published 2014. ISBN 978-1-118-54956-8

Building Dependable Distributed Systems
By Wenbing Zhao
Published 2014. ISBN 978-1-118-54943-8

Binary Decision Diagrams and Extensions for Systems Reliability Analysis
By Suprasad Amari and Liudong Xing
Forthcoming 2014. ISBN 978-1-118-54937-7

Quantitative Assessments of Distributed Systems
By Dario Bruneo and Salvatore Distefano
Forthcoming 2014. ISBN 978-1-118-59521-3